"Prof Wilson chronicles her rise ...
expert in neuropsychological rel...
that will appeal to professional c...
their families, and all others who...
Jill Winegardner
Rehabilitation, Neurological Institute, University Hospitals,
Cleveland Medical Center, USA

"In this book, with characteristic honesty and charm, Barbara A. Wilson tells the story of her full and varied life and her unparalleled career in neuropsychological rehabilitation. It documents missions to retain and develop new clinical services and brings about paradigm shifts in assessment and rehabilitation for people with brain injury world-wide, achieved through a combination of intellect, pragmatism, care and determination, with the unwavering support of Barbara's husband Mick and family, and despite deep personal tragedy through the loss of their adult daughter Sarah. There is nobody quite like Barbara, and no book quite like this one. I recommend it most highly."
Jessica Fish, PhD, DClinPsy, St George's Hospital
and King's College London, UK

"In these memoirs, Barbara A. Wilson OBE traces her remarkable life from her disadvantaged childhood through to her professional achievements, many awards, and highest honours. Professor Wilson, one of the most well-known and highly-respected clinical neuropsychologists, recounts an inspirational career dedicated to improving the lives of people with brain injury. The book also contains moving accounts of the grief and subsequent personal growth that occurred after the untimely death of her daughter and highlights the marvellous adventures of a 'serious traveller'. Written with great candour, honesty and passion, the book integrates her life with the social milieu of the time."
Robyn L Tate, Professor Emerita,
The University of Sydney, Australia

"Professor Barbara A. Wilson has inspired countless people around the world who have sought to better understand, assess and manage the consequences of brain injury. Barbara's compassion, determination and intellectual rigour are clearly reflected in her academic papers, books and her teaching. But in this deeply personal, honest account of her life, Barbara tells us about the people, experiences, challenges, successes, failures and tragedies that have shaped her as a person. Her story is fascinating, not just because it helps understand how she became one of our greatest ever neuropsychologists, but because it is story of overcoming adversity, of courage, love, and resilience in the face of devastating loss. This is a book not just for those who know Barbara or know something about neuropsychology, it is a book for anyone who wants to be the best they can be, whatever the obstacles that life puts in the way."

Jon Evans, Professor of Applied Neuropsychology,
University of Glasgow, UK

The Story of a Clinical Neuropsychologist

From a disadvantaged childhood to becoming one of our best-loved clinical neuropsychologists, this exceptional book tells the life story of Barbara A. Wilson, who has changed the way we think about brain injury rehabilitation.

Barbara's story shows how it is possible to have a fulfilling career alongside a successful family life, even when faced with the deepest of personal tragedies; the death of her adult daughter Sarah. Clinical and neuropsychologists will recognise Barbara's influence on rehabilitation practice and her tireless aim to get what is best for people needing neuropsychological rehabilitation. It will inspire those with brain injury and their families who may struggle to make life meaningful, as well as encourage readers to stick to their beliefs and triumph in the face of obstacles.

Barbara A. Wilson has worked in brain injury rehabilitation for 42 years. She founded the Oliver Zangwill Centre and the journal *Neuropsychological Rehabilitation*. She has won many awards including an OBE for services to rehabilitation.

Barbara at 18 months

The Story of a Clinical Neuropsychologist

Barbara A. Wilson

Routledge
Taylor & Francis Group

LONDON AND NEW YORK

First published 2020
by Routledge
2 Park Square, Milton Park, Abingdon, Oxon OX14 4RN

and by Routledge
52 Vanderbilt Avenue, New York, NY 10017

Routledge is an imprint of the Taylor & Francis Group, an informa
business

British Library Cataloguing-in-Publication Data
A catalogue record for this book is available from the British
Library

Library of Congress Cataloging-in-Publication Data
A catalog record has been requested for this book

ISBN: 978-0-367-28119-9 (hbk)
ISBN: 978-0-367-28117-5 (pbk)
ISBN: 978-0-429-29972-8 (ebk)

Typeset in Times New Roman
by Taylor & Francis Books

Printed and bound by CPI Group (UK) Ltd, Croydon, CR0 4YY

Contents

Figures

Preface by Michael Wilson

If you came across Barbara Wilson in 1970 you would have met a 30-year-old married woman, a hippy, Bob Dylan fan, and mother of three children aged 5, 6 and 7, married to a school teacher, living in rented accommodation, owning no house, no car, not even a fridge! Her family was struggling. Things were about to change in 1971 however, as she was about to start "A" Level Psychology, the first year in which this subject had been offered at this level in England.

Meeting her nearly 50 years later, she is a clinical neuropsychologist who has worked in brain injury rehabilitation. She has published 27 books, 201 peer-reviewed papers, 123 chapters and 8 neuropsychological tests. She has won many awards for her work, including an OBE from the Queen in 1998 for services to rehabilitation, and five lifetime achievement awards: one from the British Psychological Society, one from the International Neuropsychological Society, one from the National Academy of Neuropsychology, one from the Encephalitis Society and one from the NHS 70-year anniversary parliamentary awards where she was regional champion for the Midlands and East Region. In 2011 she received the Ramon Y Cahal award from the International Neuropsychiatric Association. In 2014 she received an honorary degree from The University of Cordoba, Argentina. Also in 2014 she received the M.B. Shapiro award from The Division of Clinical Psychology (affiliated to The British Psychological Society) for Distinguished Contributions to Clinical Psychology. In 2019 she received the annual award from the Spanish Clinical Neuropsychological Society. She is editor of the journal *Neuropsychological Rehabilitation*, which she founded in 1991, and in 1996 she established the Oliver Zangwill Centre for Neuropsychological Rehabilitation. A rehabilitation centre in Quito, Ecuador is named after her. She is currently president of the UK Encephalitis Society and is on the management committee of The World Federation of Neuro Rehabilitation. The UK Division of Neuropsychology has named a prize after her, the

"Barbara A Wilson prize for distinguished contributions to neuropsychology". She is a Fellow of The British Psychological Society, The Academy of Medical Sciences and The Academy of Social Sciences. She is honorary professor at the University of Hong Kong, the University of Sydney and the University of East Anglia. She has held 30 research grants. Her work has resulted in changes in clinical practice. For example, as a result of a randomised control trial evaluating a paging system to improve the everyday functioning of people with memory and planning problems, the local health authority set this up as a health care system for people throughout the United Kingdom.

This book is about how Barbara achieved all this and includes an accompanying account of her private and family life, her extraordinary travels round the world, her clinical work and her teaching. This autobiography starts by going back to her childhood during the Second World War when she lived in Brixton, London and had to mother her own mother who was learning disabled. Not the most promising of starts to a successful career one might think! Barbara describes her less than outstanding school career at Grammar School, her meeting with Mick and her marriage, which has lasted 57 years so far.

In an issue of *The Neuropsychologist* published in 2019, Barbara was referred to as:

> one of our best-loved and most awe-inspiring neuropsychologists … when she was honoured with a Lifetime Achievement Award as part of the Parliamentary Awards to mark the 70th anniversary of the NHS at the Houses of Parliament in July 2018. As people will be aware, Barbara is a tireless supporter of the NHS. In 1984 she led the first successful occupation of an NHS facility to prevent the illegal closure of Rivermead Rehabilitation Centre, and in 1996 she founded the Oliver Zangwill Centre for Neuropsychological Rehabilitation, the first based on the holistic model in the UK, where she works to this day.

Readers of this book will learn much about a leader who is indeed "best-loved" and "awe-inspiring" who has been a rebel "occupier", a "tireless supporter" and a "founder" of health institutions in her aim to get what is best for people needing neuropsychological rehabilitation.

Preamble

This book is a combination of personal and professional accounts of how I came to be an eminent clinical neuropsychologist specialising in the rehabilitation of survivors of brain injury. I describe my disadvantaged childhood, with a learning disabled mother, and my ultimate success through education, aided by my marriage to a supportive partner. I first went to university as a mature student at the age of 30 when my third and youngest child started school. I describe my education from graduation to PhD and my early career at Rivermead Rehabilitation Centre in 1979. It was at Rivermead when I first became intrigued by the lives of brain injured people. From the very first day there, I knew I would remain in brain injury rehabilitation for the rest of my career. Readers will learn about the fascinating lives of brain injured people and about the rehabilitation they receive in order to make their lives more manageable. They will learn about my travels in over 100 different countries, many of which I lectured in and worked with specialists in the field of neuropsychological rehabilitation. They will learn about scientific research and collaboration between professionals as well as the actual clinical work by therapists and psychologists at patient level. The book highlights the trials, triumphs and honours of my professional career interspersed with the personal story of my marriage, and friendships; and will include the death of my firstborn child, Sarah, in a white water rafting accident in Peru when she was an adult, and my subsequent travels through the extraordinary landscape of remote parts of Peru in order to reach the scene of her death in the deepest canyon in the world, the Cotahuasi. The book concludes with life after Sarah's death and after official retirement, when I continued to work as both a clinical neuropsychologist and a writer.

Part One

1 Early life

Wartime years and primary school

I was born in 1941 during the Second World War. My father was away fighting in France and my mother, who lived in south London, had to travel out of London to give birth because of the danger of bombing. Consequently, I was born in Tunbridge Wells, in Pembury Hospital. I was only there for three weeks, however, and then we moved back to London where I spent much of my childhood. Although a full-term baby, I only weighed four and a half pounds and was always told I looked like a skinned rabbit when I was born. It seems that my mother had a difficult forceps delivery and the right side of my face was squashed in. I put my poor visuo-spatial and musical skills down to the fact that I sustained some right hemisphere damage at birth.

My earliest memory is of being in a vehicle at night with what I now believe were laurel leaves brushing at the windows. I was alone and frightened. No one could have known about my fear and the leaves brushing against the window so could not have told it to me over the years. My mother said later, that at the age of 2 or 2½, I was taken from Belgrave Children's Hospital to an evacuation home in Sussex. Now I believe the vehicle was an ambulance and I was being taken from London to Sussex. My mother did not come to the evacuation home with me even though I was so young. She had, I believe, arranged the evacuation through an aunt of hers. I remember the woman I stayed with was unkind to me. I recollect two horrible things she did. She always pushed my head under the water when she was washing my hair, which terrified me, and when she went out shopping she would neither let me go with her and her children, nor would she let me stay in her house. I had to wait by the wall in front of the house. I do not remember anything about her husband or her children, just these two things she did to me. I must have been no more than 3 years old at the time. When I was older and talked to my mother about this period, she said that she was in hospital in London and heard two women talking about this little girl who was being badly treated and she realised it was me. The village I was in was near Horsham so it is not clear how these women knew the story. According to my mother, she went down to the village and had me moved to the care of another woman, who was kind to me. I don't remember anything about the second evacuation home.

I returned to London in 1945 before my fourth birthday in October, so I must have been in Sussex for about two years. I assume my mother kept in touch but this period is very vague. I remember that my father returned home at the end of the war seriously wounded. He was in a hospital outside of London and my mother, my Aunt Dot (my father's older sister) and I went on a bus to see him. We took some strawberries and I remember Dot and my mother being very excited that they had found these strawberries, which, I believe, cost them a great deal of money, at least it was a great deal for our poor family. I was eager to see my father and had convinced myself that he would have a wooden leg.

When we reached the hospital my father was in bed with a splint on his leg. I was allowed to feel this through the blanket covering him and it confirmed my belief that he would have a wooden leg. He did not, of course, but he later told me that he won a five pound bet for being the man with the most war wounds in the hospital. At one point he asked me to go and talk to a man further down in the ward (I think he wanted to speak to my mother alone). I went to talk to this man who started to cry. My dad said afterwards that the man's wife and child had died in the blitz (the bombings in Britain during the war) and I may have reminded the man of his dead child.

My dad came home and for a long time his wounds meant he needed help. My mum had to cut up his food and help him dress. He had scars everywhere including many stripes like scars across his arms. He tanned easily but these scars always stayed white. He also said he was the only person with four belly buttons; one was his natural one and the other three were from gunshot wounds to his stomach. Stomach problems plagued him for the rest of his life and he could only eat bland foods. As an adult, I cooked him a meal with garlic. He ate it but was very sick afterwards. His favourite meal was haddock with poached egg, which I thought was horrible. For many years my dad had nightmares about the war and would start screaming in the night. At one time we lived in a single bedroomed flat in Camberwell, which I shared with my parents, and these nightmares woke me up. My dad said frequently, "I am living on borrowed time." So many of his friends and comrades had been killed that he felt he should not have survived. He sometimes said "Harry (or Tom or someone) came last night." This person would be a soldier my dad knew who had been killed. He said this was evidence of ghosts but my dad was such a sceptical man and an atheist that I am not sure he really believed in ghosts. Today, I think his problems would be recognised as post traumatic stress disorder but this term had not been invented then.

One of my earliest conversations with my dad was about bananas. I had heard of bananas but never seen or eaten one. "What do they look like?" I asked. He said something like, "They are long and thin with yellow skin, white inside with a black part running down the middle." My father craved a banana but they did not sound too pleasant to me. Because eggs had been hard to come by during the war, we were supplied with dried egg powder. This came in large circular tins; the powder was mixed with water and then cooked. The result looked something like an omelette. I believe it was because I was used to dried egg powder that I never developed a liking for real eggs. I never eat boiled, poached or fried eggs although occasionally I will eat an omelette. Our food during the war was rationed. Each person was allowed so much butter, sugar, milk and so on each week. Ration books were allocated to people to enable them to purchase their allocated amount of the foodstuffs. The ration books were of different colours (for different products) made of a stiff, rough paper. They had tickets in that were torn off and given to the shopkeeper in return for the goods. We had an adequate but not luxurious diet. I remember being sent to a nearby shop with a ration book to get something for my mother and I lost the ration book. What a disaster. My mother was distraught. I do not remember the resolution of this catastrophe, only the terrible anguish of my mother. Nowadays I think she should not have sent a 4-year-old shopping alone!

My father's taste in food may have been bland but my mother's was not. She had grown up in Bristol, a seafaring city with many foreign ships and access to food and had eaten exotic foods since she was a young child. (Incidentally one of the boys she claimed to know was Archibald Alexander Leach, later named Cary Grant, who was a bit posher than everybody else and would insist that one day he would become a film star!) My mother loved snails, for example, which many British people find repugnant. We lived in Brixton, a very cosmopolitan part of the world even then in the 1940s. (Another name drop is that of David Bowie who later lived in one of the streets near us also in Brixton.) We had neighbours of many nationalities particularly West Indians, Nigerians and Cypriots. Because of this we had access to foreign foods long before the rest of London did. One of my mother's favourite foods was dried salted cod. This was purchased as a very hard sheet of dried fish, which needed to be soaked for several hours. My father called it "toe rag". I ate some of it but it was very salty so I never ate very much. There was one little shop in Brixton market that I loved. It was owned, I think, by a man from

Eastern Europe. From the ceiling hung long sausages and there were barrels of fish in brine. At this time such shops were virtually unknown and the word "delicatessen" never heard. The herring in the barrels cost four (old) pence each and one or two of these was a special treat for me. They were a little like the roll mop herrings of today but much tastier. The smells and sights of this shop impressed me as a young child. Brixton market has always been special and I remember the clothes of the Africans, the accents of the Jamaicans and the fights that would break out between the Cypriots and the local white people. There was racism, which was most evident on a Saturday night when the fights broke out and also evidenced by the KBW (Keep Brixton White) signs painted on the walls. Mostly, the different nationalities stayed in mini ghettos: for example, the West Indians lived in Somerleyton Rd and Geneva Rd. Thank goodness things have changed, a little, in the twenty-first century and overt racism is now a crime. I changed later, realising how awful racism was when I was at grammar school, aged about 12 years. I was spouting the racist remarks I had heard in Brixton when I realised the whole class had gone very quiet, I then realised that one of our class mates was black. I had never thought of her as black before. She was just a girl like the rest of us. I felt terrible for her and at what I had done; from that moment on I have hated any kind of racism.

Until I was 9 years old I had to go to hospital at least once a year with ear infections and ear abscesses. I remember terrible earaches, trips to the doctor and to Belgrave Children's hospital in South London. The National Health Service began in 1948. Before this, when I needed a doctor my mother would be worried because she did not know how much she would be charged and whether she could afford it. I also remember having to go to convalescent homes after I came out of hospital. I am not sure whether I really needed to go or whether my mother persuaded the authorities to take me to give her a break. I did not like the convalescent homes and, in particular, I did not like the condensed milk on bread we were given for tea.

At the age of four, soon after returning from Sussex, I was in a shop with my mother. She was being given some change and I could not understand how she knew the change was correct, it seemed too difficult. I remember thinking, "Maybe I am backward because I can't work this out." Obviously I was not backward and I taught myself to read before I went to school. I would ask my parents about letters on cereal boxes and on the shops we passed when taking the bus or the tram. I learned the letter "W" because we regularly passed "Woolworth's". My dad and his sisters read avidly. All three were intelligent but uneducated. They liked debate and discussion. My mother did not read books and obviously had a learning difficulty: nowadays I believe she had a phonological loop deficit and could only retain two items in immediate memory; she would have made an interesting single case study. She always said she did not learn to walk until she was six and wore leg braces and went to the "silly school". She had problems with writing. All her letters were capitals and she did not understand about punctuation. She loved singing, however, and had a wealth of songs, which she sang to me regularly. I realised from the age of about eight that I was cleverer than her and would sometimes take advantage of this. She also had a significant hearing problem and wore a hearing aid that would frequently whistle. Yet she was the kindest person, who would always help, was very supportive and loyal and I know that she and my father loved me despite sometimes showing benign neglect.

Before I started school I went to a day nursery, as my mother worked full time as a waitress. The only thing I remember about this nursery was that they made us lie on camp beds in the afternoon to rest. I had not rested during the day for as long as I could remember and I resented it. My first school was Stockwell Road Primary; I started there just before I was 5 years old. I remember some visitors coming soon after I entered the school and the teacher asked me to demonstrate my reading skills to them. They seemed to be impressed. I liked school but did not stay there long as we managed to rent a flat in the Lewis Trust buildings in Camberwell. This was a council flat for which we paid six shillings and three pence a week (just over 31 pence in today's money!). Even in those days (1947) this was incredibly cheap and was recognised as being in a rough part of the world – although I did not realise this at the time. One advantage was that the flats were opposite a bus garage, which became a playground when I was a little older. The other advantage was that there were plenty of children around so there was always someone to play with. My mother found a child minder there, Mrs Ryland, whose daughter Sylvie was the same age as me. My earliest memory of my hatred of potatoes comes from this time. Mrs Ryland regularly gave me potatoes which I could not eat. I remember dropping them down the back of her sofa. My aversion remains to this day.

At school I developed a reputation as a clever but rebellious child. As my father was a rebel, I think I inherited this streak from him although not always in the same ways. He was left wing politically and remembers having stones thrown at him when he marched for the young socialists in the 1920s. He would not let us stand up for the national anthem as he was against the royal family. He used to say "I would not let the queen use our lavatory," and I had a visual image of the queen coming to our door saying, "Please can I use your lavatory?" with my father saying a stern

"No." He had been christened a catholic and his family were from Ireland two generations back but he, himself, was a convinced atheist. My Aunt Dot was, too. She would say, "I would love to believe, it would be comforting but I can't." My mother was from a Quaker family and more conventional, although I felt her belief system was a mixture of religion and superstition.

My primary school teachers were religious and adored the royal family. Because I loved and admired my dad, conflicts were bound to arise. One day I was talking about religion at home and my father said, "There is no such thing as god." Of course, I went to school the next day and said this to the teacher, who was horrified. She called in the headmistress, who decided to ask my mother to come to the school. My mother, being a conventional soul, agreed with the teachers, thought I should never have said such a thing and scolded me. I, too, knew that the teachers would be shocked, but I liked the idea of shocking them. Later, when I was in my last year at this school, in 1953, Stalin died. My father had some admiration for the Russians because of the way the Russian soldiers had fought during the war and we did not know at that time all the terrible crimes Stalin had committed. So my dad had some sympathy for the Russian regime. About a year before this, King George the sixth died. I was at school when this happened. The headmistress came into our classroom to tell our teacher, Miss Foster, that the king had died and they both started to cry. I was amazed at their behaviour and that evening told my father. When Stalin died, I remembered this and said that it wasn't mentioned at school even though the head and the teachers had cried over the death of the king. My dad said, "Nobody cried when Stalin died did they?" Being the rebellious child I was, I repeated this sentence back at school the next day and, once again, shocked the teachers.

NOTE: During the Second World War there was a tremendous admiration and deep respect by the British for the Russians, for all they had suffered at the hands of the Nazis; it was recognised that their massive war effort was possibly the chief reason for the defeat of Germany. In Jean Lucey Pratt's (2015) wonderful autobiography about the Second World War, for example, she wrote (11 March, 1942): "saw a film recently in which Churchill and Stalin appeared. For Churchill – a few polite claps; for Stalin – a roar of applause".

Both my parents worked full time. My father was a painter and decorator and must have recovered well enough from his war wounds to return to work quite quickly. He seems to have changed jobs fairly regularly because there were times when my mother would be very anxious about whether or not he would find a job quickly. On a few occasions we looked out of the window to see him coming home and my mother could tell by his walk (or maybe by the things he was carrying) if he had lost a job or, on other occasions, if he had managed to find a job. We did not have much money but we never seemed desperately poor and there was always money for presents at Christmas and birthdays or to go to a museum or to Southend on bank holidays.

The war was a constant topic of conversation. I remember my father talking about his "demob" suit (all soldiers after the war were given a demobilisation suit) and, at some point, six war medals arrived. I have already mentioned the nightmares; another aspect of the war which affected my father for the rest of his life was shrapnel (bits of metal from bombs) that had embedded themselves in his body. Every now and again a piece would work itself through his skin. I remember a particularly nasty piece coming through quite close to his eye. If I remember rightly, he received compensation for these bits of shrapnel that emerged from his body. He spoke about the war frequently and said that once he swapped shifts with a mate; he was doing his mate a favour but the mate was killed and my father survived. Nowadays, as I said before, he would be diagnosed as having "post traumatic stress disorder". He certainly had flashbacks, intrusive thoughts and nightmares.

There were times, however, when I was left on my own for long periods. My parents would sometimes go out at night leaving me alone. I was often left alone during the day too when they had to go to work (and presumably Mrs Ryland could not look after me or my mother could not find a child minder). She would leave my lunch (or dinner as we called it then); this would be eaten pretty much straight away. I spent hours playing with paper dolls, living in an imaginary world. I also had a plan in case my parents never came back. This was to walk round to Aunt Vi's to tell her what had happened. Her house was within walking distance and I knew how to get there. At about this time I started to pretend I had an imaginary family with many brothers and sisters and pets. I called these imaginary times my "pretends" and whenever I was lonely or unhappy I would escape into my "pretends". This lasted until I was 18 and left home! We were not allowed pets in the flats and I had to wait until we moved before I could have any.

We then moved to Foreign Street (which has now been demolished) in Loughborough Junction, which is halfway between Brixton and Camberwell. We had the basement flat with my Aunt Vi, her husband Uncle Arthur and my two cousins, Peter and June, living above us. Living in Foreign Street was a good time for playing outside. Halfway up the road were some bomb ruins (houses which had been bombed during the war) where I collected milkweed and dandelion leaves for my pet rabbits. There were other bomb ruins further afield and these made great adventure playgrounds for the neighbourhood children. If these existed today, children would not be allowed to play in them for health and safety reasons but we thought they were wonderful and we had a freedom my own children and grandchildren have not had. There were also lots of other children in our street and in the adjoining streets. I remember a little girl from a Polish family called Yanny (I think her name must have been Janina). She was a tomboy and I liked her. She had lots of brothers and sisters and I believe the family was considered rough, that is, even rougher than the rest of us. My two good friends from school, Irene Storrar and Christine Trayling, lived in the next street. At the end of the road was a little corner shop called Sledmar's, known to us kids as Sleddy's. We spent our pocket money there on sherbet fountains, pear drops, aniseed balls, humbugs and the like.

In the school holidays, my cousins, Peter and June (known as Juney) and I were packed off to one of the parks for the day with sandwiches. We sometimes went to Myatt's Park, the smallest and the least interesting. Mostly we went to Ruskin Park, which had a paddling pool and swings. The furthest away, the biggest and to me the most beautiful, was Brockwell Park, which I loved. I could pretend it was the real countryside. It also had an open air swimming pool but we could only go there if an adult was with us. When I was older, and allowed to have a pet dog, I spent ages with my dog, Dusty, in Brockwell Park, which I found to be a soothing place that calmed my mind.

There was always some tension between my mother and her sister, Vi. I know Vi did not like me and I believe she did not like the fact that I passed the eleven plus and went to grammar school while her two children, Peter and Juney, did not. They both went to the technical school. They were clever enough but did not pass the examination. Vi was more competent than my mother and more successful in her own eyes. I am sure she thought my mother was a bit of a fool. My mother liked Peter and Juney but Vi did not like me. She looked after me once in my last year at primary school, when I was 11. My mother had to go to hospital for a few days. I stayed in our flat at night because my dad was home from work but Vi gave me meals during the day. In a quiet, unobtrusive way she would try to upset me. For example, when I was about to take Dusty out for a walk, she would wait until I had his lead on ready to leave, when she would stop me saying I had to have my tea. She insisted. I hated having to make the poor, excited dog wait, but she was bossy and won out. Even worse happened one hot, sunny day during the weekend just before my mother came back from the hospital. In the summer, if it was warm, both boys and girls played out with no tops on. I started to develop my breasts early and by the age of 11 had buds. Of course, this meant that I would not take my top off when I played in the street. It was embarrassing and one was subjected to ridicule. On this day, however, Vi forced me to go out topless and I hated her for it. I have never forgiven her. She was mean to me but in a secretive way.

My mother liked Peter and June and they would spend ages in our flat. My mother, June and I once went on holiday to Hastings. We stayed in a bed and breakfast and had a good time. I think I was 9 years old and June was 8. There was a sea wall there and I liked to run along the wall and jump over the cracks. Once I was so engrossed in my game I almost jumped over the end of the wall, and I pulled back at the very last moment. If I had continued to run I would have fallen from the end of the wall and almost certainly been killed. On another day we were playing in the sea near to the shore. There were big rocks embedded in the sand, which were good for jumping on and off. The tide started to come in and the rocks were becoming covered by the sea. I began to return to the shore when I noticed a little boy, probably about 3 years old, on a rock, screaming. He could not get back. I picked him up and had a struggle to reach the shore. He was quite heavy and I had to manoeuvre round the rocks. I would not let go, however. I managed to reach the shore and put down the little boy who found his parents. Nobody had seen or noticed that I had rescued him.

I went to various activities such as piano lessons, Brownies and dancing classes. My mother harboured hopes of me becoming a pianist and I persevered with the lessons for a while. The best thing was the piano teacher's cat, which sat on the top of the piano. When the teacher used a stick to point things out to me, the cat played with the stick and tried to catch it with her paw. This made me laugh. One day I decided I had had enough of the piano lessons and on the way home I hid my books in a bush, went home and told my mother I had lost them. She was cross and said, "You go back and find them and don't come home until you do." I did find them but she let me stop the piano lessons after that. The Brownies was fun for a while. It was held in a church in Wren Road (named after the architect Christopher Wren) and I loved the building. The best thing about Brownies was going for three penny worth of chips afterwards. The chips, hot and salty, tasted wonderful. I argued with Brown Owl though over something and decided to leave. Chips I could eat if they were thin enough and did not have that awful potato texture, which made (and still makes) me gag.

Dancing classes were a little more successful. After trying a tap dancing class, I joined a ballet class and did well. At the age of 11 I was in performance at the Brixton Empress. In the dressing room before the show, I twirled around to make my skirt stand out, tripped over someone's vanity case on the floor and fell face forward onto an enamel sink where I broke my two front teeth. The two inside parts fell out so that I had a missing triangle in my front teeth. I was shocked and felt it was my fault for showing off. I must have participated in the performance, although I don't remember it, but when I went home I did not want my mother to know about the broken teeth as I thought she would tell me off. Trying to hide my mouth, I hardly spoke for three days; my mother thought I was ill. Eventually I told her what had happened and was taken to the dentist where they filed the rough bits of tooth and said they could not crown the teeth until I was 18 years old. That was the end of dancing for me.

When I was 9 years old, I entered a competition in the local evening paper to win tickets to go to the Festival of Britain. There was a children's section in the paper called Squibbet (named after an imaginary animal that was half squirrel and half rabbit). Contestants were required to answer a number of questions and, thanks to my father who helped me with a couple of them, I was one of the winners. I had to sign a form saying no one had helped me and, to this day, I feel guilty about lying! The Festival of Britain took place in May 1951. There were three main parts, the Skylon (a big tower), the South Bank Festival Hall and Battersea fun fair. I won three tickets so went on three separate days with my mother and my Aunt Dot. I found the Skylon and the South Bank boring but I loved Battersea fun fair. We returned several times. The Skylon no longer exists but the South Bank Festival Hall is still there and I have been to several concerts and plays over the years so my views have changed.

This was before the age of mass television and we listened to the radio all the time. My two favourite programmes were *Dick Barton, Special Agent* and *Journey Into Space*. My dad and I listened together. I first saw a television picture when I lived in Lewis Trust buildings in Camberwell. The father of a girl I knew, called Beryl, had a TV set and allowed some of his daughter's friends to go to and watch this for a few minutes. We saw a flickering picture on a screen; I can't remember what the programme was about, but I remember thinking it was boring and I did not see television again until Coronation Day on 2 June, 1953. My Aunt Vi had bought a TV set for this occasion and we spent some of the time watching it. Even though my dad was anti-royalist, my mother was not. Again, it was very boring. On Saturday evenings we often went to Vi's to watch TV. *Saturday Night at the London Palladium* was another programme I found tiresome. Soon after this we purchased our own TV. One of the results of this was that my father spent more evenings at home. Before we bought the TV he had gone to the pub every night but now went less often.

Two other events which stay in my mind happened around this time. Just before the coronation was the conquest of Everest, another big event in our lives. We were especially taken with Tiger Tenzing, the Nepalese Sherpa who helped Sir Edmund Hillary and his team to the top of the mountain. The other thing that happened was that Roger Bannister broke the 4-minute mile with the help of Chris Brasher and Christopher Chataway. This was considered a huge achievement, discussed at length by my dad.

I was a popular person until I went to the grammar school. Most of the other kids went – or would eventually go – to the local secondary modern school, Cormont Rd, which had an awful reputation. I was no longer welcome among the neighbourhood kids once I had passed the eleven plus and I led a different, more solitary life.

2   Grammar schooldays in south London

I went to Charles Edward Brooke Grammar School for Girls (CEBS). It was a church aided (Church of England) school. After I passed the eleven plus, my parents and I had to select three grammar schools and hope I was accepted at one of them. My parents left all the decisions to me. I knew that the most desirable schools, Mary Datchelor and James Allen Girls School (JAGS) would almost certainly not accept me – they would, I thought, consider me too common. I also knew that I would probably be accepted at CEBS: besides, my cousin Ann (my Aunt Dot's daughter) went there, and I liked the driveway up to the school! I told my mother to put this school first, with Mary Datchelor second and JAGS third. My mother and I went for an interview at CEBS, where one of the questions I was asked was: what did I want to do when I left school? I said I wanted to be a farmer's wife. The head mistress was surprised and said didn't I want to be the farmer? This was the first glimmering maybe about equality for women that I had heard. I had never faced sexism but took it as read that my place was to be a farmer's wife.

I started at CEBS the school in September 1953. My first best friend was Pamela Remmet, but she was expelled soon after so I became best friends with Mary Lambert and remained so until we left school at the age of 18 years. Mary's father was a waiter at the Café Royal and her mother, a Scottish woman, was interesting with a sharp sense of humour. Both Mary's parents were clever and self-educated. I liked CEBS and did well there.

Most years I won a prize, usually for English. Our English teacher was Miss Phillips, a thin, grey-haired woman who made us learn one poem every week as part of our homework. I loved doing this and learned many poems, some of which I still remember word for word to this day – to the amazement of my husband. Some poems were traditional ones from books supplied by the school, like Tennyson's "The Eagle" and Walter De La Mare's "The Listeners". I still enjoy these poems in my late seventies.

Other poems, though, were ones I had found out myself through my dad or through Mary's family. My dad told me of an Irish poem about a dog called Tray and I managed to find this poem (long before the days of Google) and learned this for homework one week. It began, "On the green banks of Shannon when Shelagh was nigh, no blithe Irish lad was so happy as I." This poem is called "The Harper" and is by Thomas Campbell. My dad also told me about a poem called "The Green Eye of the Little Yellow God", which I managed to find through our local library. This, too, was learned for my English homework and I loved the poem. I can still recite the whole of it today. One line, however, caused me great embarrassment at school when I recited it in front of the class. The line was "but for all his foolish pranks, he was worshipped by the ranks". I made an error though and said "but for all his foolish pranks he was worshipped by the wanks". The whole class knew what "wanks" were and I was partly mortified and partly amused by what I had said. My dad also taught me the words to "Kevin Barry", an Irish rebel song, but I never recited that for my English homework! I think I had learned a bit more sense since leaving primary school. More poems were gleaned from the books in Mary's house. Her parents had a whole range of *Punch* volumes with funny poems in and I sometimes chose one of these to learn for my homework. One, for example was called "The Twins", which I found highly amusing, and another that made my father laugh was called "The Vulture" by Hilaire Belloc.

Another teacher I remember well was Miss Curphy, our geography teacher. She was very tall, came from Liverpool and smiled a great deal. She was less distant than the other teachers and the girls felt she enjoyed our company. One wet lunch time, in the third year, we were in our classrooms killing time until the afternoon lessons started. I drew an outline of the British Isles, from memory, on the blackboard. Miss Curphy came in later, saw the map and asked who had drawn it. I said it was me. She did not say anything then but later that year I was awarded the geography prize. I am sure it was because of my drawing on the blackboard.

The teacher I respected most was the maths teacher, Miss Green. She was a short, sturdy, fierce looking woman, very strict but considered fair. She once insulted us by calling us "gutter snipes" but I felt she liked me. Although English was my best subject, I did pretty well at maths. I particularly enjoyed algebra and geometry because of their problem-solving elements. Our Latin teacher was also very strict, I have forgotten her name but she was Scottish, black haired with a sharp tongue. She once saw me writing my initials, "BF", on a book and said, "If I had initials like that I wouldn't advertise them." It was the first time I realised that my initials stood for "Bloody Fool". I was so embarrassed and never forgave her for humiliating me so but from then on I always used my middle initial "A".

Holidays were always part of my life. My parents and I went somewhere on most bank holidays, frequently to Southend. We usually had an annual summer holiday too. As a tiny child my mother had taken me on at least two occasions to visit a distant relative, Aunt Margaret, who lived on a farm near Perth. We travelled by coach and I was horribly travel sick. I loved the farm though and helped collect the eggs and shoo the cows away if they came too near the house, something my mother was too scared to do. Once I was put on the back of a working horse and I remember my legs sticking out sideways as they were too short to go down the sides of the horse. I felt as if I were in heaven.

During my time at CEBS we often went to Butlin's Holiday Camp for our summer holiday. We liked our trips there although I would never dream of going to such a place now, preferring more up-market places. We took the train and my dad was brilliant about finding us seats. He would climb in the first class carriage then rush back to third class and

Figure 2.1 Barbara aged 8 in fancy dress

grab three seats while my mother and I boarded with the third class passengers. We entered many of the competitions at Butlin's such as fancy dress for me, knobbly knees for my dad and singing contests for my mum. I don't remember winning any competitions but one day we won a bottle of champagne. Each evening at dinner, there was a huge circular board with table numbers round the edge and a dial that could be spun. One of the staff would swing the dial and wait until the hand stopped. The table number closest to where the hand stopped won a bottle of champagne. One year our table won the champagne. My first real crush was on one of the redcoats at Butlin's called Bernie, I thought he was just gorgeous. One year we took Mary with us and she had a good time too but when we told one of the teachers where we had been on holiday she said to Mary, "I didn't think you would holiday at places like that." I realised that she thought going to Butlin's was common and after that I felt embarrassed to tell people where we went.

Mary's mother had another sister, who lived in Slough, and we often spent weekends there. We spent whole days exploring the surrounding countryside by bike. I borrowed the aunt's bike and Mary borrowed her uncle's. I remember the freedom and exhilaration of these trips well. Although I lived in London, I always felt that inside I was a country child and loved being in rural areas. We explored Runnymede, Virginia Water and Stoke Poges where Thomas Gray wrote "Elegy Written in a Country Churchyard", so I learned this poem for my English homework too.

My first trip abroad was to Norway when I was 16. I had a Norwegian penfriend, Gro Foyn, and wanted to visit her. My parents could not afford to pay for me so I sold a litter of puppies to fund the air fare. At that time it was cheaper to fly at night so I booked a night flight to Oslo at the cost of £31. I went for Christmas. My cousin Ann, came with me to the airport. I was really scared of going alone but was determined to travel. Gro met me at the airport in Oslo and we went to her house in Elverum where she lived with her parents and her younger sister, Berit. Gro's father was a forester and my surname was Forester. He was amused by this. The family was very kind to me and seemed to like me even though I was so unsophisticated. We visited people in the village to wish them happy Christmas, Gro told everyone I lived in London as if this were a magical city. People were impressed and everyone gave us a marzipan pig, which I thought was charming. On Christmas day, I became a little exuberant, put on Per Foyn's homburg hat and sang "Maybe it's because I'm a Londoner". Mr and Mrs Foyn were so amused they called in the neighbours for a second rendition.

Gro was the school champion skier; Mr Foyn's work was completed on skis in the winter and the whole family were excellent skiers. I went skiing with them and wasn't very good. I could not learn how to stop when going downhill. The only way I could be sure of stopping was to fall over. One day we were going down the biggest hill in Elverum. I was not doing too badly but felt I was too fast and had to keep stopping. I did not hurt myself but I broke my watch on one of the falls (I did not ski again until I was 60 years old, when I tried to learn cross country skiing in Colorado). I wanted Gro to visit me in London but her mother was too scared to let her come. She thought London was a very dangerous place where people were murdered every day.

My next trip to Norway was 18 months later when a school friend, Jean Smith, and I went by train and ship. Jean had a penfriend in the same village so we both went to stay. We took the train to Newcastle and then the ship to Oslo and another train to Hamar, near Elverum. The crossing was rough and we were terribly sea sick on the ship. We had a cabin and I could not decide whether I felt worse there or on deck. At that time, knee-length white socks were all the rage in England; Jean and I wore them throughout our journey to Norway. When we were not being sick we noticed that people kept staring at us and some Norwegian boys chased us. We could not work out what was happening. It was the same on the train journey from Oslo to Hamar; we were stared at and noticed people laughing at us. When we reached our destination and Mrs Foyn met us, she gasped in horror and made us change our socks immediately. Apparently knee-length white socks in Norway at that time were worn by prostitutes! No wonder we had been the focus of so much attention on the way out! Jean's penfriend told us that they had not known whether Jean would turn out to be a boy or a girl as they thought Jean was a boy's name. It is in France, of course, but not in the United Kingdom.

I said earlier that I sold a litter of puppies to fund my trip to Norway. This was a pedigree litter from my first pedigree dog – or rather bitch. When I was about 15 I became seriously interested in dogs. I bought *Our Dogs* and *Dog World* every week and started going to dog shows. Mary sometimes came with me. I remember going to a Bulldog show once and a woman bought us each a coffee to "encourage young people to the breed". My favourite shows, however, were the big championship shows like Crufts and Windsor. I particularly liked the exotic hounds such as Afghans, Salukis and Borzois. I once saw a Borzoi on a bombed ruin site in Brixton. I talked to the woman with the Borzoi and she was a Russian émigré from the time of the Czars! Soon after this we had to write an essay for English homework called "Beauty in unexpected places", so I wrote about the Borzoi amid the willow herbs and the bombed ruins. I received a good mark for that essay as I did for one called "Making friends", when I imagined a Martian coming to earth and not understanding that smiling was a friendly gesture.

Anyway, back to dogs. I did not go out much in the evenings, instead I would sit and pore over dog books. I spent my pocket money on books about dogs, going to Foyles in the Charing Cross Road most Saturdays to browse among the books and decide which one I would buy next. My parents agreed that I could buy a pedigree dog, so I saved for that. I could not decide what breed to buy at first. I knew an Afghan or Borzoi would be too expensive and too inappropriate for our house and small garden. I also wanted to show and knew that I should avoid a breed requiring lots of trimming as I did not have the expertise; I also realised that if I went for a popular breed, the big breeders would win out. Eventually, I decided on a Manchester Terrier as these were not expensive to buy, there were very few entered at shows (indeed they had almost become extinct a few years earlier) and I had a chance of winning. I contacted a breeder in Lincolnshire and arranged to buy a bitch puppy. I sent her a cheque for £25 I believe and the puppy arrived at Kings Cross station in a box. I collected the puppy, feeling very sorry for her cooped up in a box, but when we arrived home in Brixton she was fine and friendly. Dusty was happy with her and my dad said she was lovely. Her pedigree name and the one she was registered with at the Kennel Club was Hallgarth Romance but we called her Debbie.

When she was older I showed her, with a little success – a few rosettes and third prizes. I wanted to breed from her, so when she was about 15 months old I took her back to Lincolnshire to be mated to a dog recommended by the breeder. My mother came with me to Kings Cross and went to buy my ticket. On the train I showed the ticket to the ticket collector and then looked at it myself. My mother had bought me a single instead of a return! I did not have enough money with me to purchase a return ticket; I was still at school so did not have a cheque book and had no means to pay for my fare home. I was fretting about this all the way to Lincoln and had no choice but to tell the breeder what had happened. She loaned me the money and I sent her a postal order the following day. The mating was successful and Debbie had six puppies, I kept one and sold the rest to pay for my trip to Norway. I registered my own kennel name, Cottonwoods, with the Kennel Club and registered all six puppies. Each was named after a film; Cottonwoods Shiralee was the name of the one I kept, although at home we called her Tumbleweed. One day, when Debbie was nursing her puppies, she started to twitch violently. I called the vet, who came to give her an injection. Apparently she was short of some mineral but recovered immediately after the injection. The vet asked me if I would like a job working with him as a veterinary nurse. I thanked him but said I was hoping to go to college. Tumbleweed, too, had a little success at shows but no first prizes. During one of the shows I heard about an American dog imported by a breeder in the West Country. The dog was called Eaglespur Sir Oscar of Chatham Farms and I decided that Tumbleweed should be mated to him for her first litter. Other breeders at the shows were saying it was too big a risk to "breed out" i.e. to mate to a sire with no genetic links to the bitch. I thought Oscar was a handsome dog and was prepared to take the risk. I went by train to Worcester, with a return ticket this time. I stayed the night with the breeder, Mrs Knight, and her husband. They lived in a most beautiful house and took me out to a grand restaurant for dinner. I was embarrassed because I only had scruffy clothes. They ignored this and treated me very graciously. I remember entertaining them with stories about my pet hedgehog that I had bought at the pet shop near London Zoo. This hedgehog was very tame and followed me around. To entertain visitors, I would walk down the street with the hedgehog following me. The dogs were frightened of it as it nipped their paws if they went too close. Not long after this though the dogs killed the hedgehog and I went home from school to find it dead.

Tumbleweed mated successfully with Oscar and in due course gave birth to a litter of puppies that I helped to deliver. Tumbleweed started having her puppies while I was at school and my mother didn't know what to do so she phoned the headmistress to ask if I could go home. The headmistress came into the class where I was at the time and said, "Your dog is having puppies and your mother doesn't know what to do. Please go home." I went home to find only one puppy had been born so I was there for the birth of the other five. When one male puppy came out I said to myself that he would be a champion. We could not keep him at home with our small garden and two bitches so my father's friend kept him but he was registered and shown in my name. He was called Cottonwoods Boomerang and later went on to win best of breed at Crufts – my proudest moment in the world of dog showing. However, when I entered the dog at the next championship show, I learned that he had been killed. My father's friend had let him run the streets and he was killed by a car. I lost heart in dog showing after that.

3 Marriage, babies and being a hippy

When I left school I went to teacher training college at Bognor Regis. I chose this college because I read that it had an equal number of men and women so I thought I stood a better chance of getting a boyfriend there! I chose the career because I had seen a film about the education of a deaf girl: the film was called *Mandy* and it had a big effect on me. I decided that was what I wanted to do, teach deaf children, but I had to qualify as a teacher first. I applied to Bognor and went for an interview. I remember I had to read a passage in which there was a conversation between country folk. I put on a West Country accent to read these conversations and this raised a smile from the woman interviewing me. I was accepted at Bognor and started in October 1960. On arrival, a group of six of us were shown around by a second-year student, a young woman. A man called Mick Wilson, another second-year student, came over to our group and invited us all up to his room for coffee. The young woman showing us around said, "Mick Wilson never does that." We went for coffee and, whereas everyone else was given a normal sized mug, my coffee arrived in a giant beer mug. This was the man I was eventually to marry, but at the time I was completely unaware that he was making a statement. There was a dance at the end of the first week and all first years were paired with someone of the opposite sex from the second year to accompany them to the dance. My partner was a tall, lanky guy but at the dance Mick Wilson persuaded this man to let me go with him instead. My room mate, a quiet girl who was easy to get on with, said that Mick Wilson really liked me. I could not believe this and said, "I think he has confused me with someone else."

Mick had already been at the college for a year and was in fact nearly seven years older than me. He had, as they say, been around a bit. At college he was noted particularly for his sporting ability and eventually obtained coaching certificates in football, cricket, swimming and life saving. I remember seeing him hit 89 not out in one cricket match when he played for Broadstairs, and for much of our early married life he played football for teams like Marks Tey in Essex, and once had a trial for Margate town. Early on I was struck by Mick's generosity. We'd been going out for only a couple of weeks when he took me to town to buy me a pair of shoes. And he would treat me to the cinema. One of the first films we saw together was the Bolshoi Ballet Company's production of *Giselle*. I think he had been able to get labouring work during the holidays and he spent some of the money he earned on me! In fact, Mick, later, throughout our marriage, has always been keen to shop with me for clothes and his final choices have nearly always been right! I remember one occasion, looking ahead to the 1960s, when we went to a clothes shop in Colchester and I was trying on a dress in one of the cubicles. Mick was hanging around when a shop assistant rushed by saying, "We need some fresh air in this place," and proceeded to squeeze a can labelled "Freshe Aire", which released a spray around the room. This was such an odd thing to do in those days and now of course we are inundated with chemical sprays, perfumes and cleaning materials. Anyway, this same woman then informed Mick that, "Your wife is ready for you to see her," took Mick to a cubicle, opened the curtain with a dramatic flourish only for Mick to see a strange lady posing in a bikini, not his wife at all. There was an embarrassed scuffle and a laugh from Mick.

The other great interest for Mick was jazz, particularly Traditional New Orleans style, and this has remained a passion for the whole of his adult life. He played trumpet in what he described as the worst band in the world, the Bognor college band, and later in our marriage he got into the Kennet Jazz Band based in Reading. However, Mick did play with some really talented musicians who understood chords and could improvise. Mick claims he stayed in the Kennet Band because he was the one who collected the money at the end of the gig. Mick always admitted he had little talent for music but he could get by playing trumpet lead because all you needed to do was play the melody!

In many ways I did well at Bognor; I took an exam which placed me in the top group, I did a good first teaching practice but had a stormy relationship with Mick. He was my first serious boyfriend and the one who introduced me to the joys of sex. We were both left wing with similar views on politics, education and religion. However, he was over six years older than me, very experienced and mature and I was convinced he was going to dump me. This belief was so strong and I was so unsure of myself that I decided to finish with him first. At the end of the first year, my life was in a mess and I attempted suicide with some drugs I had been given. I survived, was sent home, and went to Bethlem Royal Hospital as an inpatient. I realised while there that I was not the same as the other inpatients and I did not believe I had a mental illness. In order to obtain my discharge I knew I had to tell the doctors what they wanted to hear, that is that I had a mental illness. I was discharged, have had no mental health problems or treatment ever since and for many years kept the fact that I had been an inpatient at a hospital (where I was later to work) a secret. When I left the hospital, I was expecting to return to Bognor Regis training college, the hospital was expecting this too, but Bognor refused to have me back. Despite protesting this decision, I was unable to return.

So there I was, at home, unsure what to do. I went to an agency looking for au pair work overseas. I applied to go to Baghdad! It was not such a dangerous city then. While this application was being processed, I happened to be walking down Oxford Street when I saw Mick's sister, Gloria. I had met her once or twice when I had been going out with Mick. Neither Gloria nor I recognised each other at first, we looked at each other and walked on, only realising who the other person was after we had passed on. Apparently, when Gloria arrived home she told Mick that she had seen his ex-girlfriend, Barbara, in Oxford Street. Mick phoned me at home that night. My father answered the phone and said, "That Mick Wilson's on the phone. Do you want to speak to him?" My parents blamed Mick for the suicide attempt although, of course, it wasn't his fault. I agreed to speak to Mick and he invited me out to a Chinese meal in Denmark Street in a couple of days' time. I said to myself, if I go out with him, I will end up marrying him. In fact Mick had telephoned me from a telephone booth in the narrow avenue between Charing Cross Road and Denmark Street, and when I agreed to meet him he too said to himself that eventually we would marry. He also said he cried in the booth. I didn't cry.

Two days later we went for the meal and he told me he was a working at a school for deaf children in Margate and he could get me a job there as a house mother. This sounded better than going to Baghdad as a nanny so I agreed and became a house mother at the Royal school for deaf children in Margate.

In many ways, this school, in those days, was not a good place for the young children being taught there. Very young children were taken away from their families, signing was forbidden so many of these children had no means of communication and we were encouraged to be strict. Some of the people there were good. I worked there for six months, marrying soon after at Ramsgate Registry Office with just two witnesses. We went on the train to London from there to go to my parents who provided a meal. At the station a strange woman rushed up to Mick to hug him; this was his youngest sister, Carol, who became one of my best friends. We had a very unpretentious meal at my parents' and the following day we hitchhiked to Cornwall, with camping gear, for our honeymoon!

We found a field in which to camp in Trebarwith, after obtaining permission from the farmer. Having set up camp, we went for a walk along the cliffs. We were climbing up, with Mick in front. I was aware of a large amount of green slime and was worried in case this made Mick slip. I kept reminding him to watch the green slime when, suddenly, I slipped on it myself! At first I thought I would come to a stop, so was not too concerned, but then I went over the edge of one of the cliffs and felt as if the ground were rushing up to meet me. I remembered my father saying when you need to relax pretend to be an old sock so I told myself "pretend to be an old sock". I must have fallen about 20 feet, landed in a shallow dip on the beach, and spun round. Somehow Mick had scrambled down the rocks and was by my side in no time. He thought he would be married to a disabled person forever while I was more worried about drowning, so I stood up. I appeared unhurt apart from a nasty cut on the back of my head, which bled profusely. We walked along the beach and my memory is that everyone turned their heads away from me. Certainly nobody offered to help. We went to a local doctor who checked me out and said scalp wounds did bleed a lot so not to worry. We returned to the camp, Mick went to the town to get some provisions while I stayed behind rather shaken. For some reason I decided to do some washing, I think I wanted to feel like a housewife so I started washing Mick's underwear. I was sitting on the ground with a bowl of water in front of me when I went into a muscular spasm; my back went rigid and I fell back onto the ground unable to move. It was probably a late result of the fall from the cliff. I lay there until Mick returned when his first thought was "My god, the farmer has raped her!" I explained what had happened and he went to call an ambulance.

Eventually the ambulance came and I was strapped onto a wooden plank and spent an uncomfortable journey to the hospital. Mick came too with the camping gear and camped in the grounds of the hospital where he survived on Cornish pasties for several days. I took a book with me, it was F. Scott Fitzgerald's *Tender is the Night*. One of the nurses saw it on my bedside table and, knowing it was my honeymoon, said, "It won't be very tender tonight, dear!" Both Mick and I thought that was very funny. There was nothing seriously wrong with my back. I stayed in hospital for three or four days and was then discharged. I was rather stiff and could not carry my rucksack so Mick took them both and we caught a train back to London. It was not the best of honeymoons but at least I was not permanently disabled.

Mick was working at The Royal School for Deaf Children as a teacher. I did not have a job and was rather miserable. We found a lovely house to rent in Broadstairs, very close to the famous Bleak House described by Dickens. We joined CND (The Campaign for Nuclear Disarmament) and became friends with Alan Kemp who owned the Albion bookshop in Broadstairs. Very soon after we had settled into our first home at Broadstairs I went shopping in the town centre, and amongst other things, bought myself a science fiction book entitled *Level Seven* – a title that is forever imprinted on my mind. On Mick's return home from Margate he picked up the book while I was in the kitchen and began to read it – without my knowledge. After dinner we decided to go to bed and, with the lights still on, Mick picked up my book and continued to read from page 59, which he had reached at his first reading. I was taken aback at this and remonstrated that it was the book I had bought that very day and I wanted to read it! Mick expressed his disappointment at having to give up a book that had absorbed him from the beginning. As I began to wonder was this going to be the first big row of our marriage, Mick came up with a suggestion (so shocking to us now as we like to think of ourselves as book lovers) to tear out the first 59 pages and that I would read these as he continued to read from page 60 onwards and that he could continue to tear out further pages as and when necessary! We actually did this with more than an element of smugness that overwhelmed any proper sense of guilt.

The story does not end there. We began to read and it was not long before Mick noticed I was reading a lot faster than he was. He started to read more quickly and, as I caught on, so did I. It became obvious that I was a faster reader than Mick and we reached the ignominious position for Mick when he had to hand over the book to me and from then on I would tear out the pages to hand to *him*. Many years later Mick admitted to me that this silly interlude had left a big impression on him and that he realised then that he had married someone who was possibly a more able reader than him! Although of course fast reading is not necessarily a measure of any profound cognitive ability!

I became pregnant within six weeks of marriage. Despite being rather poor and saying we would wait for a while before having children, I really wanted this baby. I looked very young, having always looked younger than my years. This was the really bad winter when it snowed from Boxing Day 1962 and did not thaw out until 21 March 1963. I used to walk along the beach with the wind blowing, looking so much like a pregnant child that people stared at me. Once Mick and I went to look at a flat to rent and the woman who answered the door said to Mick, "Do you have any other children besides this one?"

We've never spent much time in the snow in our 56 years of marriage apart from that very first year of the big freeze. We were living in the

Garden House in Broadstairs. It was a pretty little house tucked off the main road and surrounded by neat gardens all sheltered from the main thoroughfare. Our very first home, remembered now, as well as the snow, for the pretty little black cat we called Geronimo, whom we lost after about ten weeks. I was desperate and went looking for Geronimo for days calling his name in all the gardens but he didn't show up until we put an advertisement in the local newspaper. The people who had looked after him brought him back and informed us that they had called him Sooty, which horrified us! People must have thought this young woman was mad calling for Geronimo as she walked around the gardens! We had gone back to Mick's parents' for Christmas and returned to the Garden House two days after Boxing Day. As we approached the house we could hear the rushing of water and when we opened the front door, water continued to cascade down the stairs and onto the front path. Although Mick had turned off all the taps in the house before leaving, he had forgotten this one tap in the upstairs lavatory and the water had continued to spill since Boxing Day. It was so bad that the water had completely filled the cellar under the stairs to its very top. Luckily for us, the house was built upon chalk and the huge cube of water drained away within three days. However, the dampness remained with us for the rest of the several months we lived there.

One other thing I remember is my twenty-first birthday party held in the Garden House. Mick had invited Mel, one of the teachers at the School for Deaf Children, to the party and he, being a rugby player for Thanet, decided to bring the whole of his team to the party. As we opened the door to them our hearts lifted from their immediate gloom when we saw they were each carrying a bottle of spirits. However all of them turned out to be filled with water. Mick never forgave Mel! That big freeze has always been remembered and remains famous for the fact that there were even icebergs in the sea off the north-facing beaches of Margate. Mick was working in a primary school in Birchington, after he left the school for deaf children, and he remembers cycling to school in the same wheel ruck from January to March with his beard frozen to his face! He would come indoors and peel the ice from his beard.

Other snowy landscapes remembered in our marriage were experienced as a result of our travels in Finland, Alaska and Colorado. In Finland we spent a day visiting a famous house named Hvittrask, then having become a museum to honour Finnish architects from a firm called Gesellius Lindgren and Saarinen. It was located 19 miles from the west of Helsinki near a place called Kirkkonummi, and it was genuinely beautiful, being filled with wonderful examples of Art Nouveau furniture and ornamentation, including some exceptional wood-burning stoves with extraordinarily coloured ceramic chimneys. We had arrived early after trekking the last two miles from the railway station and we had the house to ourselves in the very early morning, so silent except for the wind blowing outside and the snow falling and swirling round the windows. There was also a lovely walk through the snow to a sauna by a lake in which, we were told, the locals swam during the summer months when wild blueberries grew on the wooded slopes.

In Alaska we were driving one day through some quite heavy snow and the only other vehicles were the snowmobiles of hunters. Mick and I got out of the car for him to take a photo of me against a particularly snowy backdrop. We had left the car engine running and the door closed on Mick's side and we realised we were locked out of the car – and in danger of being frozen to death! One or two of the hunters came to see if they could help but, like us, were confounded by the locked doors on both sides and the key in the lock as the engine continued its merry chugging! The only solution, it was agreed, was to smash one of the widows and climb in to open the doors. This was not as easy as it would seem when Mick kept throwing a rock as big as a fist at the selected window. It wouldn't break and we realised later that breaking a car window in this way was so foreign to Mick that he could not exert sufficient strength in his throws. Eventually Mick's hesitancy was overcome and the window was smashed. With an article of clothing stuck haphazardly round the window we spent the rest of the journey trying to shelter from windspeed and showers. Thankfully, the car hirers were entirely sympathetic and we did not have to pay for the broken window!

Our final snow adventure took place in Colorado, in the United States. We had arranged a four-day holiday at a ranch called "Vista Verdi" near Denver Springs and it snowed for the whole time we were there. Five feet of snow fell in four days! Our stay seemed magical in its vastly deep and growing depths of snow filling the meadows and slopes and piling on top of buildings; together with the lovely, warm comfort that waited for us indoors when we were entertained in the evenings, around the log fire and after hearty steaks, by visiting cowboy musicians who played for us after exceptionally hearty meals. During the day we were taught cross-country skiing and Mick, who kept falling on his backside, was angrily irritated by the fact that I was better at it than he was. He kept saying it was because I was short with a low level of gravity – whatever that was supposed to mean? I just kept smiling!

One of the most exciting adventures for us at the ranch was a sledge ride we took, pulled by eight huskies. The owners had almost called the ride off because of the unusual depth of the snow and poor visibility. However, they let us go because there would be two or three accompanying snowmobiles and riders from the company alongside us. What could possibly go wrong?

It was decided that I would be lying on the sledge, wrapped in blankets, watching the dogs in front of me, and Mick would be standing on a wooden bar at the back of the sledge holding on to two handles, one on each side at chest level. Mick was told to control the dogs by shouting "Mush" to calm them and slow them down. Well, that didn't work. We charged off with the dogs apparently pulling as hard as they could to speed though the very deep snow. As far as I was concerned it was a lovely ride: I was warm and I loved the way the dogs charged ahead, barking loudly, slowing down on up hills and rushing like mad down hills. I couldn't see Mick, in fact I forgot all about him, letting myself go with the flow, speeding through the dark snowbound landscape. The snow-mobiles soon broke down as they couldn't get through the unusually deep snow. The dogs had no problem! We were on our own with them in an Arctic-like landscape. They seemed to know where they were going so I was quite relaxed. I could hear Mick occasionally shouting "Mush" but it didn't seem to make any difference: the dogs were enjoying themselves, barking like mad. One of the best rides of my life!

On arriving at the end of the ride, which the dogs seemed to know automatically, I turned excitedly round to smile at Mick and expected him to smile back at me. He, however, was hardly able to stand up, was as pale as the snow and could not say anything. Apparently, it was extremely difficult for him to remain standing on the wooden bar and on several occasions he slipped off and was dragged through the snow holding on to the handles with all his might. Then he would have an easier time when the dogs slowed down going up the hills and he could scrabble along through knee-deep snow. The worst times were when the dogs rushed downhill. It was so bad at these times that Mick said he was holding on to the handles with his body levitating horizontally, trying to shout "Mush" to no avail. I didn't know what to say as I basked in the afterglow of my ride, covered in warm blankets, loving the dogs, remembering the smooth movement through the snow. We never did find out what happened to the snowmobiles and their riders.

So, now I will return to the early days of our marriage but I want to inform the reader at this point that, although this autobiography will read approximately chronologically, I will be side tracking at times to include memories that come to mind and seem to fit.

Later we moved to another lovely rented house in St Nicholas-at-Wade, where I spent a lot of time cooking and knitting. I also went to a Russian evening class and learned the Cyrillic alphabet. It was at this class that I went into labour. Sarah, our beautiful firstborn daughter was born in Ramsgate General Hospital. Being small, the staff were worried about the size of my pelvis and made me stay in bed. I knew I

Figure 3.1 The second year of our marriage – with Sarah. As a 22-year-old mother, Barbara still had difficulty getting into pubs!

needed to walk around and keep moving but I wasn't allowed to and ended up having a caesarean section. The baby was fine however. I saw the job satisfaction on the faces of the midwives when a healthy baby was delivered and wanted very much to become a midwife. This never happened although I did deliver my second granddaughter many years later as we will see. We both loved baby Sarah from the start and went home after ten days. Mick always shared in the childcare and was a very modern man despite being born in 1935. I think this was because he had a strong mother and three powerful sisters.

Meanwhile Mick had a new job, where he was probably at his happiest professionally. He knew that his real calling was for literature and language teaching at secondary level, and it wasn't long before he found the perfect school for him in Colchester, Essex. It was a secondary modern school that Mick dubbed "The Eton of all sec. mods."! His move there coincided with the introduction of the Certificate of Secondary Education (CSE) in the 1960s, a new national exam for pupils who for the most part were thought to be unsuited to the demands of GCE. In fact this new exam was liberating for both teachers and pupils in those secondary modern schools where the staff had the nerve and capacity to grasp the nettle by designing their own courses that could be stimulating, liberating and demanding.

In the seven years Mick was at Monkwick, I continued in my role as mother and housewife as well as working in a pre-school nursery, and later for the Government Social Survey (later renamed the Office for Population Census and Surveys and finally the Office for National Statistics). Mick, meanwhile, made a name for himself locally and amongst the county inspectorate as a creative teacher who encouraged development of language and learning in the classroom. It was the 1960s and there was considerable interest among educationalists in the process of learning through pupil participation and creative writing. In those years Ted Hughes was in charge of some BBC schools' programmes, David Holbrook had a huge influence on the English curriculum, the Rosens were having a political say on freedom to learn in the classroom, Douglas Barnes had written *Language, The Learner and the School*, many English departments in universities were busy liberating studies, Bob Dylan was an adored song writer and the Beatles were also having an effect on ideas relating to liberation and equality. David Davies, the poet, was head of English at Essex University and Mick was invited to lecture there on children's writing. Mick's own research, which he developed into a research degree at Master's level some years later, compared pupils' verbal interaction in small pupil-led groups with that of similarly sized teacher-led groups. His findings showed that while teacher-led groups scored higher in post-discussion tests (not by much and certainly not significantly in statistical terms) the pupil-led groups talked more, were hypothetical and questioning in their approach, and in the best cases spoke with a much greater degree of freedom and insight than in the teacher-led groups, which were dominated by teacher talk, lecturing and questioning. A tendency was for teachers to question pupils on ideas the teachers themselves had thought of whilst preparing the discussion material (usually a poem or prose extract), until they got the answer they wanted; the pupils would then repeat the knowledge thereby gained and do better in exams that were prepared by other teachers who thought along similar lines to those of the teacher leading the group. The pupils in pupil-led groups simply enjoyed the literature more, were quite prolific in entering into the world of the writer, asked more far-ranging questions and, above all, entered into the world of the writer more enthusiastically. Unfortunately, exams are limited in measuring the actual process of learning and concentrate more on the facts pupils have been lectured in. At a later stage I hope to quote from two of the groups to illustrate the points I have been making here. For the time being I wish to end this foray into Mick's work by quoting an article he wrote many, many years later. In 2016, in his late seventies, he wrote this piece for the *East Anglian Daily Times* in which he criticises the then Minister of Education,

Michael Gove, who decided, at a stroke, to end course work as part of the exam at GCE "O" level. The article shows that Mick had not lost any of his enthusiasm for encouraging pupils to participate in their own learning.

On September 2nd, 2012 the *East Anglian* published a story about Danish teachers visiting a comprehensive school in Suffolk. It was reported that the Danish teachers refused to believe that the UK would adopt the "backward-looking" plans that Michael Gove is seeking to re-introduce for all sixteen year olds, which will involve all pupils sitting gruelling three-hour written exams. They regarded Mr. Gove's plans as … "the surreal ramblings of an educational nutter …"

Mr. Gove's educational ideas seem to be set in 1950s concrete and do not reflect the needs of the 21st century. He is constantly referring to Britain's global requirements but cannot appreciate that these can only be met by problem solvers, not parrots. We need to encourage students to think divergently rather than simply memorising facts. Unfortunately, Michael Gove's intention to re-introduce three-hour exams and to end course work for GCSE students will put a nail in the coffin of independent thinking and creativity. Three-hour exams are totally inappropriate for this day and age. They will encourage pseudo lecturing by teachers or promote the 1950's style teaching cycle whereby the classroom teacher *structures* a situation, *asks a question*, which is then *answered* by one out of maybe as many as 30 pupils, all sitting passively at their desks or urgently raising their hands, "Please Miss, please Miss …"; then the teacher *reacts* to that answer. The trouble is that in this cycle the teacher has three moves and 30 pupils passively share one: teacher is doing all the work and pupils are not doing much more than guessing what might be in the teacher's head. Although pupils hardly get a look in when teachers "teach to the test", they cannot help but be part of the conspiracy as they, and seemingly their parents, accept that real work is copying down what the teacher says. Another problem is that this kind of whole class teaching does not stretch the very able while the less academic get left behind.

What this kind of teaching does *not* do is stimulate students to think for themselves. On the other hand, pupil-led group work that is encouraged, and is indeed necessary for course work and modular activities, encourages peer group interaction in which individual pupils hypothesise, guess, interpret, imagine, argue, disagree or agree, give opinions, and summarise: all essential tools for developing co-operation and successful work with colleagues in future workplaces. If Gove's absurd and outdated proposals are introduced we might get better three-hour exam results that may push us higher in the global classroom league table for facts and memory testing (Gove's ambition), but it won't promote an ability to solve problems.

Although Michael Gove is always going on about work in the classroom needing to be rigorous he does not understand the difference between the terms *rigorous* and *arduous*. Rigorous refers to studies that are careful, diligent, painstaking, thorough, studious, and – above all – pleasurable: it refers to the kind of *active learning* that goes on when a student is working on a piece of course work of which he or she is proud. It is this kind of work, usually kept in folders and portfolios and frequently displayed in classrooms to the student's peer group, that Mr. Gove wants to end. It is this kind of work when a pupil has time and interest and commitment, that Mr. Gove wants to abolish. It is this kind of work that certainly professional adults do almost every day and therefore is best applied in classrooms as preparation for 21st century quick wittedness in the global market. Yet Mr. Gove wants to end it! In its place he wishes to re-introduce arduous three-hour exams at the end of two years' memorising.

"Arduous" refers to work that is taxing, onerous, laborious, burdensome, relentless, fatiguing, grinding, intolerable. You know, when your brain is numb, your fingers inky, and your wrists ache with *passive* note taking in preparation for a three-hour exam to be taken in a year or two's time.

Course work is frequently completed by pupils, who might at times be working together, i.e. *co-operating*, or using the whole range of modern media to investigate an hypothesis; while solely preparing for an exam is associated with solitude when an individual is silently *competing* with others. If Mr. Gove's aim is to create masters and docile workers he's on the right lines.

Problematically, many adults believe that the old way of examining makes results fairer and more reliable but three-hour exams after two years of study are extremely poor at recognising talent: they are taken on one day and can only cover a small number of items. A different set of questions taken on another day could produce a different result. Assessment over two years, combining written course work, assessment of oral contributions in class, *and* a final written exam give a much more complete and accurate picture of a candidate's abilities. Although it is true that course work assessment is problematic because thousands of teachers do the marking, such assessment is becoming controlled better and, if teachers were enabled to go into each other's schools to monitor and compare marking systems, as they were with Modes II and III CSE courses in the 1960s and 70s, greater fairness could be achieved. It should also be noted that GCE style exams are marked by many different examiners, leading to their own lack of fairness and accuracy.

Course work, which Gove intends to abolish, encourages greater participation, commitment and achievement. Standards in writing, spelling and grammar are much higher when a pupil has the chance to alter, re-write and improve written work that will be kept in folders and frequently displayed to fellow pupils in the classroom, and maybe even illustrated with care and pride. One-off writings seen by only one or two examiners and thereafter lost forever have not gone through the essential process of re-shaping for a real audience: the peer group in the classroom, teachers, and the family. Sitting a three-hour exam one has no time to re-draft or re-shape in order to make one's views, opinions and even knowledge of facts more readable. You just don't have time to check spellings and grammar, and get things right! Not a good preparation for a professional workforce. I not only pity the next generation of fifth formers who will have to sit these exams but I also sympathise with future employers who will be faced with an examination lottery that has such little validity in the modern world.

Mick Wilson

I was pregnant again and this time when I went into labour, I spent the evening walking round the flat we were renting in Maldon Road, Colchester.

In the morning I said we needed to go to Lexden Maternity home where I was booked for another caesarean section the following day. It was about one and a half miles to walk there from our flat and every time I had a contraction, I would stop to pee behind a bush. We reached the hospital and Mick took Sarah to the nursery where we had booked her in for a short time. Meanwhile I had the baby naturally and easily. This was Anna and she was the easiest birth of our three children. When Mick returned to see me he said, "Has anything happened?" I told him I had had the baby and all was well. He could not believe this as he had been so sure I would need another C-section.

My parents were both still alive then, although my father had been diagnosed with lung cancer and was very ill. He had met Sarah before he had one lung removed and we have a lovely photo of my dad holding his grandchild. After the lung was removed, however, he was never really well. I saw him in hospital and he said how much pain he was in. He came home, very thin, and was told he could not return to work until he put on more weight. He tried to do this and took some powder called

"Wate-On" but that didn't help. He would walk down the road and become so fatigued that he had to sit on a wall to rest. He was embarrassed at this and thought people would think he was drunk. The cancer metastasised, it had spread to his brain and his stomach. He had radiotherapy, which caused him to lose his hair and to become aphasic for a time. He hated this. He had always been a decent looking, smart man and now looked like a hobo. After Anna was born, I went to see him every two weeks. At first he was home and then he went into The Whittington Hospital where he died in January 1965. Anna was four months old; he had never seen her and would never see his grandson, Matthew. The last time I saw my father, he was in hospital. As I left, I said I would see him in two weeks to which he replied that he would not be here then. It was obvious he knew he was going to die and, had I been more mature, I would have talked to him about death and dying. Instead I said, "What do you mean?" My father realised I wasn't ready to talk about death and said he meant that he would be moved to another hospital. We both knew that is not what he really meant and I have never forgiven myself for not giving him the opportunity to talk about dying. I talk about death very easily now since Sarah died but then I was just too green. My dad died a few days later, in many ways it was a relief because his suffering ended.

Back to our life in Colchester. Before Matthew was born, I was walking along Maldon Road one day with my two daughters when a woman with two young children stopped me and asked me to join a women's discussion group. They met weekly in the woman's house, her name was Lotte, and she wanted me to join them. I was scared but went. Most of the women were university wives and Lotte's eldest child, Naomi, was just a little older than Sarah so for the rest of our time in Colchester Sarah and Naomi became good friends. This was my first time exposed to the university world and it probably sowed the seeds of my belief that I *could* go to university.

The third, and last baby, Matthew, arrived 17 months after Anna's birth in April 1966. He was born at home in Brook Street, Colchester, the first house we bought, a very small terraced building in a distinctly working-class area that skirted the town centre. I wanted this baby at home and thought it would be as easy as Anna's birth, but during one of the contractions the baby's heart stopped. Our doctor was called but the heart started again and, in the end, the birth was fairly straightforward. Matthew, however, was almost a cot death when he nearly suffocated himself in his pram and then he almost drowned in the paddling pool so he was always a bit of a worry. Now, though, he is a famous photographer living in Chile. More about all three children will be written throughout the book. At that time we had three babies

Figure 3.2 A typical 1960's portrait photo of Barbara, who was pregnant with Matthew at the time, taken by Bernard Watson – a talented artist and photographer, clarinet player in one of Mick's bands; also, conscientious objector who worked down the mines instead of fighting in the Second World War. Missed terribly by Mick.

under 3 years old; there were no disposable nappies so we were always washing, soaking, rinsing or drying nappies.

The main advantage of the house in Brook Street was that it had quite a large garden and so Mick took up vegetable gardening in a big way. This was something that has lasted all through the years of our marriage until quite recently when Mick reached the age of 79 and the actual physical work involved became too much. Mick's gardening has meant that for most of our married life we have enjoyed vegetables that have been completely free of chemicals, and we loved going into the garden to pick fresh lettuces, potatoes, beans, onions, carrots, cabbages, marrows and many more in the late afternoons prior to cooking them. My life was taken up by caring for the family of three children and housewifely duties involved in running the household and feeding everybody. This caused much strain and some depression as my mind was not being stretched at the same time as my brain was calling out desperately for stimulating activity. I did find a job the following year. The three children were all at the same playgroup in Colchester and I was fortunate enough to find employment for two days a week there.

One memory that sticks in my mind from this time was to do with the guinea pigs we kept. We had Peruvian guinea pigs, the ones with

Figure 3.3 Young mother in the 1960s, reading to Sarah, Anna, Matthew and
friend Naomi

long fur, and we all thought they were pretty and amusing. When baby
guinea pigs are born they can run immediately and look a little like
clockwork toys. One night all but one of our guinea pigs were killed,
we think by a badger as there were curved claw marks down the cage –
quite unlike a fox's claws. One baby guinea pig born that night survived, however, and I found it the next morning. Of course, we were all
very sad but I tried to do my best for this new baby and looked after it.
It became imprinted on me and treated me as its mother. It followed
me around everywhere I went and at night it slept in the pocket of an
overall I hung on the end of the bed. When I needed to be sure the
baby would not get trodden on, I put it in the overall pocket. At
playgroup, when the children were sitting in a circle on the floor, I
would walk around with the tiny guinea pig trotting after me. At first I
was enchanted by the little creature who thought I was its mother but
the enchantment wore thin after a week or two. Our neighbour, two
doors away, had guinea pigs and I persuaded them to adopt our little
one. For a few days all went well until the same creature that had killed
ours repeated the job with the neighbours' guinea pigs and they were
all killed including my "adopted" baby!

It was a bit of a struggle working at the playgroup with my own three there at the same time but first Sarah and then Anna started school and I was to find another job. I saw an advertisement for the Government Social Survey in London for which employees conducted surveys around the country. I went for an interview, was accepted, then did some training in London before starting on my first survey. We employed a local woman to help with the children and the house and I felt much happier going out to work in a job that stretched me a little.

We loved our three beautiful children, they were always well dressed in "hippy" clothes. We did not own a house (having sold the Brook Street house), a car, a washing machine or a watch at that time. We were hippies who were inspired by Bob Dylan, who was born the same year as me (a few months earlier), and his first LP came out the year we were married, so he has always been an important part of our lives. My mother was alive then and loved her grandchildren. She sometimes took the two girls on holiday and visited us from London regularly. We also travelled; not having a car, we went on public transport with our three children, our cats in two cat boxes and our stick insects in a large, empty sweet jar. We would often go to Suffolk to visit various members of Mick's family or to camp in the grounds of his wealthy friends Mike and Sue Crooks. Occasionally we went camping in France (without the cats and stick insects) and once went with some French friends to Corsica. Life was to change, however, when I started university. Talking of the stick insects reminds me of an amusing story. I cleaned the jar with the stick insects regularly; there were little seed-like things in the bottom of the jar and I did not like to throw these away as I thought they might be stick insect eggs. I decided to put them in an empty jam jar on the window sill. One morning I came down to find miniature stick insects everywhere. They were indeed eggs and all had hatched at the same time! I retrieved them from the curtains, the floor, the kitchen utensils and anywhere else I could find them. Altogether I counted 401 very tiny baby stick insects. Some went to a pet shop and some went to the children's friends.

4 University as a mature student

As I mentioned earlier, I was bored at home before my various jobs. I loved working for the Government Social Survey and was involved in many interesting surveys. I could not accept all of them though as I did not drive at that time so just took on surveys where I could rely on public transport. Mick was still working as a schoolteacher so could help with the children and we paid a neighbour to do some child minding. I went to evening classes to "keep my mind active" and tried drama, woodwork and sociology.

We then moved to Birmingham for Mick to do an advanced teacher training qualification. Mick started his course at the university, and we settled the children into a local primary school. Matthew started school there. Within days the children had been coerced by the other children to adopt a Brummie accent. Meanwhile I wanted to start another evening class so I phoned the local technical college in Bourneville and asked if there was such a thing as "A" level psychology? The woman who answered the phone said, "It's funny you should ask that as the first psychology 'A' level in the country is starting this week. There are three pilot schemes trialling this and one is at Bourneville College. The class is held two evenings a week for 8 months. You come along." So I did, and this was the beginning of my career in psychology. I went for two evenings a week, had an excellent teacher, Colin McColl, and fell in love with the subject. Meanwhile I found another daytime job helping out at a play group. I was always good with the children and had lots of ideas about craft making, games and songs (although I could not sing in tune, I knew many songs).

At this time I published my first book. Mick was asked to do some books for Penguin Education (now defunct) on the theme of families. He wrote two books in the series and I wrote one with Charles Frisby, a teacher from Coventry. The one I did with Charles was called *Families in Other Places* and I wrote pieces on Australian Aborigine Families and

Native American Families. I did my research at the University of Birmingham library and also used the library for research for essays and experiments for my psychology evening classes. These classes were thoroughly enjoyable. Several people in the class were applying for university and I thought I was as good as any of them so maybe I should apply too. Mick, who was to move to Reading as a trainer of teachers, after the Birmingham course ended, was very encouraging about me going to university so I applied. I knew I had to apply to somewhere within reasonable travelling distance so the University of Reading was my first choice and two London Colleges of London University were my second and third. I was interviewed at each and offered a place at each but decided to go to Reading for ease of travelling.

I remember my first day there, I walked through the gates of Reading University feeling immensely proud of myself and telling myself I had made it. I loved the course, the students, the staff, everything. For me it was bliss. I thought it was easier being a mature student than a younger student. Being married, I didn't have to worry about boyfriends. Having had my three children I didn't have to worry about when to start a family, I didn't have to worry about housing as we had a decent place to live. My children were well, my husband supportive both practically and emotionally so life was good. Just before going I was told that another mature student was starting the same day as me to do English. Her husband, John, was a colleague of Mick's. This was Jo Tasker. We met for lunch at the university that week and spent hours talking together. John and Jo Tasker have been close friends to this day. Matthew is good friends with their three sons and we hold them in great affection.

Mick's job was at Bulmershe College of Education, later to become part of the University of Reading. He was a lecturer in classroom studies. Before he started he was looking forward to a post where he could use all the knowledge and experience he had gained as a teacher in a secondary modern school. However, on his return home from his first day he was crestfallen and admitted to me that he thought he had made a grave error in giving up school teaching, which he had loved for ten years. In fact Mick's new job coincided with my entry into higher education followed by a Master's degree, a PhD and my exciting professional duties as a clinical psychologist. Mick's new post in higher education and my entry into an exciting intellectual world were the major turning point of our married lives. From now on my career was to take precedence and Mick's was to fall gently away as he became more involved in looking after the children and running a household. This was done with no regrets and happened very smoothly: I started a career which was to become highly successful and merited many awards and honours and Mick supported me throughout. I believe he was a Modern Man before the expression was invented!

We were still hard up and I worked in the holidays. At the end of the first year, I worked in Mars chocolate factory in Slough (a bus took us from Reading each day). It was a mind-numbing job. I was packing a type of chocolate called Revels. I can still feel the shape my fingers made as they filled the boxes. I used to make up games to pass the time; these would be such things as how many packets would I have to put in to complete a box and how many of this, that and the other would happen before the next break. At the end of the second year I managed to find a job in Heelas (a John Lewis store) in Reading selling men's underwear. On my first day, the manageress said if you have to measure a man don't do it from the front in case he gets an erection. Do it from the side! Another thing I realised was that if you asked some of the men what size underpants they needed, most did not know but some would say something like, "I take a size 8 hat" or, "My shirt size is 34" or something along those lines. Hat or shirt size has nothing to do with size of underpants of course. Needless to say, I did not tell any of the people interviewing me that I was really a university student.

By the time I was in the third year, I realised I wanted to pursue a career in clinical psychology. I was investigating how to do this and saw that one needed to gain relevant experience as an assistant psychologist or nursing assistant or something similar for several months in order to be accepted on a clinical psychology training course. Being a mature student and wanting to get on with my career, I thought I needed to find a way round this so I applied for a job at Borocourt Hospital, what was then called a subnormality hospital. I worked there for six months as a nursing assistant on night duty for two nights a week while still attending university. I worked the 8.00 pm to 8.00 am shift and sometimes had to go straight to university after I finished in the morning. It was really tough. The work was a mixture of fascinating and awful. There were some interesting patients, including one little boy who was 14 years old but never grew and seemed like a baby. There were patients who smeared faeces everywhere, there were patients having frequent seizures. Usually there were two staff working together at night trying to sort all the problems out but occasionally I was on my own dealing with this. One night two senior members of staff came to seek my help as the patients on one ward had climbed into each other's beds and nobody know who was who. I knew some of the patients and could help a bit but by morning we were still unsure we had everyone back in the right bed. Presumably the day staff were able to do this. The one thing that kept me going was the realisation that I did not have to do this for ever. Plus, of course, knowing that this would count as relevant experience. The point to bear in mind here is that I was doing all this extra work at the same time as I was studying and heading for a first class honours degree in Psychology!

Meanwhile I was applying for places to train as a clinical psychologist and my first choice was the Institute of Psychiatry (IOP) Course in South London. This had a good reputation but was next to and part of The Maudsley and King's College Hospitals. King's I had attended several times as a child when I had accidents, and as for The Maudsley, we always called this the mad house. As children, we ran past it as fast as possible. Furthermore, Bethlem Royal Hospital, where I had been an inpatient after my suicide attempt, was a sister hospital to The Maudsley and in the same hospital trust. So this was part of my early home patch. I knew I had to keep quiet about my time in Bethlem in case it spoiled my chances of acceptance. I wondered if they would find out I had been there but I knew that I was admitted under my maiden name and was now applying under my married name so thought that maybe it would be all right. I decided to take the risk of saying I had not had a mental illness and it worked out well in the end.

The other advantage of applying for the IOP course was that the Medical Research Council gave scholarships for some of the students and, short of money as always, I was hoping for one of these.

Meanwhile, I was revising for the final exams. Mick would often take the children away so I could revise. At Easter, he took them to the Isle of Wight and I went down one day to see them all. We were chipping stones in the hope of finding a fossil when a stone chip went into my leg and remains there to this day. Anna, in particular, was fascinated by fossils and some of her birthday trips were to Charmouth in Dorset to find them. She also bred mice and wanted to breed a blue one, so she worked out all the genetics and succeeded in breeding a blue mouse!

Apart from the occasional foray and break, I worked hard at my revision. I spent so much holiday and weekend time away from Mick and the children that Carol asked Sarah if we were getting divorced! Far from it; Mick just wanted me to do well. Examination time came and I thought I did reasonably well. I had employment lined up for the summer, working in London at some boring but well-paid job. I was there when the results came through but when I phoned Mick to see how I had done he said the results had *not* come through. This was not true, he just wanted to surprise me. I arrived home to find a big card and a bottle of champagne waiting. I had obtained a first class honours degree, the only one in my class to get a First and I had won a prize from the university for this. This meant I could take up my place at the IOP and I obtained one of the MRC scholarships, which helped our financial situation enormously.

Considering my role as a mother and wife and my various daytime and night-time jobs, Mick told me how brilliantly I had done to get a First! I can certainly say with conviction that, at least since leaving school, I have always known what hard work is all about!

After a summer working in London, I made the difficult journey to South London to start my clinical training, which involved an even longer commute. I had to do this for two years. I enjoyed most of the placements but was particularly interested in neuropsychology. The teacher there was Tony, a very talented and funny man and, *when* he turned up (which he often didn't), he was a superb teacher. He had problems with alcohol though and moved through several jobs before disappearing from the world of neuropsychology. I saw my first and only brain operation while training at the IOP. During my neuropsychology placement I was asked if I wanted to see Mr Charles Polkey operate. I jumped at the chance, thinking I might never have this opportunity again. I was at the end of my first year, and a second-year student, Val Muter, watched the same operation. Being only five feet tall, I was given a stool to stand on. I was in awe of the whole procedure. I had not realised that a drill was used to get through the skull and was shocked to see that bits of bone flew about like sawdust! I felt a little queasy but did not want to miss anything so forced myself not to be sick or to faint. Val Muter, however, fainted or nearly fainted several times. She was the one people were concerned about and sympathetic to. I was ignored and I remember thinking they were reinforcing Val's inappropriate behaviour. I believe I would be a little more sympathetic today.

While on my neuropsychology placement, I worked with a patient who taught me not to accept everything I was told. Naturally sceptical, this was confirmed and intensified after the episode I am now going to recount. There was a woman on the ward, who was, or so I was told, hysteric. She had problems walking yet the neurologists could find nothing wrong, so I was asked to treat her and improve her walking. I set up a behaviour management programme and I persuaded her to walk a slowly increasing amount each day. This was reasonably successful and she was able to walk a little way down Denmark Hill before I took a break for the Easter holiday. When I returned, I went to see her. She wasn't on the ward so I asked where she was. I was told that she had died of a spinal tumour! She was not suffering from hysteria at all. I felt bad for ever having doubted her and wasn't sure what to think of my successful behaviour programme.

I also enjoyed my training at Hilda Lewis House (HLH at Bethlem Royal Hospital (yes, the same Bethlem) where I worked with Janet Carr, Glyn Murphy and Pat Howlin, three great psychologists who taught me a considerable amount. I was less interested in adult mental health, preferring the neuropsychologically impaired people.

Two important lessons I learned at the IOP, and still remember to this day, were that every patient you see should be capable of being written up for a journal and that you have to learn to live with your failures. The first of these lessons is, no doubt, too ambitious, but it does make you think about planning treatment and writing up. The second lesson is self-evident and we all have our failures but many young people coming in to the profession feel they have to have a solution to every problem. This is not always possible of course. The training at the IOP was a science-practitioner model. We were scientists and clinicians and expected to evaluate what we do. This attitude appealed to me. From then on I have found it difficult to separate clinical work from research. If we are preparing and planning for our patients and evaluating what we do then research is under way.

My two years at the IOP passed and I had to look for a job. I really wanted to work in neuropsychology as I found the combination of normality and abnormality fascinating but no neuropsychology posts within commuting distance were available at that time. Janet Carr, Glyn Murphy and Pat Howlin, however, were looking for a junior qualified clinical psychologist to work with them at HLH with severely intellectually handicapped children. They suggested I apply. I thought about it and decided it would be a good start to my career. The post was a university post, with three days a week clinical work at HLH and two days a week teaching at the IOP. I accepted the post and began my first job as a clinical psychologist.

Janet, Glyn and Pat were excellent mentors and very soon I began to feel confident as a psychologist. The consultant was John Corbett. I liked him and felt he made things happen. In fact my first international conference came about through John Corbett. I submitted a paper to an international meeting on learning disability in Jerusalem. This was on reducing self-injurious behaviour. I started publishing papers and chapters at this time. One of the important lessons I learned was that if any child we were working with did not learn, it was our fault because we had not found the right method. It was our responsibility to find a solution, or at least a partial solution. This, it seemed, was healthier than when I first moved to neuropsychology where the prevailing attitude at the time encouraged us to believe it was the patient's fault. For example, we were taught (at least implicitly) that this man doesn't learn because he has frontal lobe damage or this woman doesn't learn because she has hippocampal damage or something along those lines. Because of my learning disability experience that it is up to us to find a solution or a partial solution, I have always felt that neuropsychology is about more than assessment and we have to find ways to help the people we are working with.

Much as I liked working at the IOP and HLH, the commuting was a nightmare. On the three days I worked at Bethlem, I spent three hours each way travelling. The children were all at school in Reading. They were in bed when I left. Matthew still remembers me saying goodbye and that they needed to get up in 40 minutes. Mick dealt with breakfast and getting them to school before going to his teacher training post at Bulmershe College, later to become part of Reading University. I caught the bus into town and then a train from Reading to Paddington. From there I took the underground to the Elephant and Castle before getting a bus to Denmark Hill and a short walk to the Maudsley Hospital. From there I boarded the free staff bus to Bethlem. The whole journey was reversed at the end of the day! The two days teaching at the IOP involved a shorter journey as I did not need to take the staff bus to Bethlem but it was still a long commute. After two years of this, I had had enough. A job was being advertised at Rivermead Rehabilitation Centre in Oxford (much nearer to Reading than the IOP and HLH). It was a neuropsychological rehabilitation post and I wanted this very much. I realised, however, that I had no experience in this field. I had been teaching neuropsychology at the IOP but it was the rehabilitation side I did not know about. I phoned May Davidson, the head psychologist for Oxford to say I was interested in the post but had little experience and was she hoping to attract an experienced person for this position? She said, the only person with experience is the person leaving the Rivermead post, Nadina Lincoln, so don't let that put you off and if Bill Yule tries to stop you applying don't let him! I applied, was successful, and started my first neuropsychology post in October 1979. Meanwhile I had learned to drive and bought a little white mini that served me well for a few years.

5   My career starts

Discovering brain injury rehabilitation at Rivermead Rehabilitation Centre

It was with some trepidation that I started my first day at Rivermead Rehabilitation Centre (RRC). I drove there in the mini and met the staff. People were friendly and I realised that my predecessor, Nadina Lincoln, was well liked and had established a good relationship with the staff there. She had integrated well, worked on cognitive and behaviour problems and had published in these areas. My first referral occurred that day, when one of the physiotherapists came to my room and asked if I would see one of the patients, Derek (not his real name), to help him lose weight. I was scared as I had never worked on eating disorders or addictions of any kind. On the other hand I did not want to admit I was unable to help as I had been taught to accept that clinical psychologists are expected to deal with whatever problems they come across. We should apply our current knowledge to any health-related problem referred to us and be prepared to alter our approach in line with developing knowledge. So I agreed to see Derek the following week. He had been coming to RRC two days a week, having been an inpatient a few months earlier. The day passed and I realised how interesting the centre was and how fascinating were the patients! I said to myself at the end of that day that I would remain in brain injury rehabilitation for the rest of my career. And I did!

How could I help Derek to lose weight? I knew that during my training one of the other students had worked in weight reduction, so that night I phoned her and explained that I was expected to help a man lose weight but I had no idea how to start. She told me not to worry and that I should start by asking him to keep a baseline for two weeks of everything he eats and drinks. Meanwhile she would send me some papers to tell me how to proceed after that. I thanked her and went to bed feeling a bit more comfortable. However, when I saw Derek, who was accompanied by his father, the following week, I could not proceed in the way I had been told! Derek had been a soldier and had received a gunshot wound to his head. The bullet had entered the left occipital area and lodged in the left temporal area. He had several operations and was infected by meningitis as well as other infections. He had significant brain damage resulting in an acquired dyslexia (he was unable to read, having once been a normal reader), a visual object agnosia (inability to recognise objects), as well as some language and memory problems. Thus he could not read or write so could not complete a baseline in the usual way. I was desperately trying to think on my feet: at first I thought to myself that I would take the baseline and Derek could telephone me every time he ate or drank anything. I quickly dismissed that idea as I realised he might be eating or drinking in the middle of the night or when I was in a meeting or at some other awkward time. My next thought was to loan Derek my dictaphone so he could dictate each time he ate or drank. That idea, too, was soon shelved as there was only one dictaphone in the department. Derek had memory problems and might well lose the machine. Then I looked at his father, realised I could enlist his help, and asked him to take the baselines. This duly happened.

Meanwhile my colleague sent papers on reducing weight and I realised that, like other areas in psychology, we just had to set an appropriate, realistic and achievable goal and find the right reinforcement. The goal was for Derek to lose two pounds in weight each week. He was attending RRC two days a week but wanted to come more often so we agreed that if he lost two pounds a week, he could have an extra day at RRC. So successful was this that Derek lost 30 pounds over the next two months. Derek was also seen for his dyslexia and this is reported in Wilson (1999). He was taught to read again to the level of a 13-year-old but he remained a letter-by-letter reader and had surface dyslexia, which meant he could only read regular words.

These were the days before funding became a big issue. In the National Health Service (NHS) at that time there existed the principle of free referral whereby anyone could be referred from any health authority and be seen for free. At RRC, approximately one third of patients came from the local area, one third came from the region and the remaining third came from elsewhere in the country. Such luxury is no longer available. There were three social workers at RRC, helping families with financial and social issues, and I could call on any one of them but, for many years now, I have never been able to seek the assistance of social workers because they all seem to be tied up with helping abused children.

I loved my days at RRC although, being the only psychologist there, I could not see everyone. I turned this to my advantage by going to ward rounds and choosing the people I thought I could help, or seeing individuals especially referred to me. I learned a great deal from the other staff. In my previous work at HLH in addition to the behaviour problems which every child had (frequently self-injurious behaviour such as head banging or eye gouging), I worked with language problems but that was not required at RRC as there were two speech and language therapists (SALTS). I sometimes worked with them as well as with the occupational therapists (OTs) and the physiotherapists (PTs). I suppose this was the beginning of my respect for other professionals working in rehabilitation and my belief in working cooperatively with them on shared problems.

For a period of seven years, while we were living in Reading, Mick started playing the trumpet again with a bunch of New Orleans Jazz aficionados: there were two architects, one on drums, one on trombone; a solicitor who played clarinet; a chemist on piano; a zoologist on banjo; and a bass guitarist whose profession we did not know although we think he worked in the Berkshire County Hall with some of the others. They called themselves The Kennet Jazz Band and played in a local pub once a week, had sporadic gigs in village halls, and on some Saturdays played in the morning at the Hexagon, a big centre in the middle of Reading. There must have been hundreds if not thousands of these local jazz bands dotted all over the UK from the mid-1950s to the 1970s, and in fact there are still some of them playing to this day, despite the fact that British pop music, when it became so wonderful, almost killed them off from the beginning of the 1960s. It is worth noting however that many of the early rock and roll musicians were influenced by the jazz bands: the teenage Mick Jagger, for instance, used to go to some of Ken Colyer's jazz band gigs held in Great Newport Street in London in the late 1950s. Others such as John Lennon and Paul McCartney started their musical careers playing skiffle – which was introduced to the UK by the Ken Colyer Band, a member of which was Lonnie Donegan, the banjo player.

Some of the Kennet Jazz Band were good musicians (Mick didn't count himself as one of these and argued that the good ones understood chords well and could improvise at will). They tried to play pure New Orleans jazz in the style of people like Bunk Johnson, George Lewis (revered men who started the world jazz revival in New Orleans in the 1940s) and Ken Colyer, Mick's favourite British jazz musician. I suppose I became a jazz widow for some of that time or else I'd go along and drink at the bar with a few other wives and girlfriends. I never really got the bug however, not like Mick who could be moved to tears of joy when listening to people like Bunk Johnson, George Lewis or – in England – Ken Colyer. I was far more stage struck by Bob Dylan, whom Mick also came to love forever. In fact, in later years, Mick and I went to the first great music festival at the Isle of Wight when Dylan was playing.

There's quite a good story about Mick's interest in jazz and it involves none other than the great film director, Spike Lee. Some time in the 1980s our son Matthew was working in a restaurant in Brighton and he got to know Spike Lee, who spent a bit of time in that town. When Mick learned that Matthew had met Spike he thought he could put two and two together and make five of an idea he had had in his mind for many years. This was a story he had compiled based upon Bunk Johnson's life, which he was convinced would make a brilliant film. Basically it was about Bunk who gave up playing jazz after one night when a man ran into the place they were performing in order to kill the drummer for stealing his girlfriend. In the chaos that followed, the stage was destroyed and several instruments were ruined. This is quite a famous story in jazz history: Bunk left town and was not seen for a number of years until two university lecturers went looking for him. They found him eventually working as a lorry driver and teaching music to children part time. The two lecturers bought Bunk a set of false teeth and through their contacts got him a trumpet donated by none other than Louis Armstrong. In short Bunk was rehabilitated, formed a new band and for a few years played some of the world's greatest New Orleans Jazz in the 1950s revival. He was known throughout many parts of the world including all of Europe, Scandinavia and countries such as Japan and other parts of Asia.

So Mick had been dreaming of this story for many years and would have loved to have been able to make a film of it that, in his mind, would win several Oscars! Here was Mick's chance. He compiled a small parcel containing his ideas for a film script, a couple of numbers by Bunk's band from a 1944 recording, and a short published biography of Bunk himself. He got our son Matthew to give this to Spike Lee, accompanied by a grovelling letter wondering whether Spike might ever consider making a film about Bunk. What a cheek! However, Spike was very nice (not minding this particular cup of English tea) and thanked Mick for bringing Bunk to his attention, pointing out also that his own father was a jazz fan and knew all about Bunk. To this day Mick lives in hope that a film about Bunk will be made by someone (and in fact there has been a recently formed Bunk Johnson appreciation society that is flourishing in New Orleans), so we shall have to continue to wait.

I began to specialise in memory problems as nobody else was doing that and soon started running memory groups. I will describe some of the patients and groups that interested me most at that time. At ward round one day we learned about a 30-year-old woman who had been admitted following an anaesthetic accident. Such accidents were uncommon then and even more uncommon now that greater care is taken, but they do sometimes happen. This woman sustained anoxic brain damage following an operation to replace a heart valve. The anaesthetic accident left her blind, dysphasic, hemiplegic and apraxic. So she could not see, she could not speak, one side of her body did not move at all, and the other side did not do what she required of it. The consultant asked me to assess her and tell the team what her cognitive functioning was like! I gulped and thought to myself that I could assess people who could not see; I could assess people who could not speak; and I could assess people who could not move but they had to do one of these things if they were to be assessed. However, I could not refuse to assess her as I heard in my head the voice of one my teachers, Bill Yule, saying, "You must never say a patient is untestable: it says more about the psychologist than it says about the patient." So I agreed to assess the woman. I thought back to my days at HLH and decided to apply the Portage developmental checklists to obtain data about the woman's functioning.

The Portage checklists, named after the town of Portage in the US state of Wisconsin, are (or were) used to assess preschool children with learning disabilities. They are designed to assess children from birth to the age of 6 years. Typically, the psychologist goes into the child's home and observes the child, with the parents, to complete the five checklists which cover socialisation, cognitive, motor, communication and self-help skills. The developmental gaps are identified and these are set as goals to work on. Instead of parents, I observed the patient with her PT, OT and SALT. Through observation with them, I was able to complete the checklists. On each list her scores came out at below 2 years of age. The first goal, as identified by the self-help checklist, was to teach her to drink from a cup alone. In some ways this was a useful way to assess her: we obtained objective, baseline data, we were able to set a realistic and achievable goal, and we were able to monitor progress. In other ways, though, the Portage Scales were not right for adults: they were designed for children and some of the items were inappropriate. For example, one of the items is "waves goodbye in imitation of an adult". Although fine for a baby or toddler, we do not expect adults to do this. Recognising the need for a new tool, similar to Portage but appropriate for adults, the recognition of our predicament was the initial impetus for the development of a new assessment procedure, which was to become the Wessex Head Injury Matrix, and I will say more about that in the next chapter.

I was sometimes asked to help with problems of challenging behaviour. Typically this would be a young man swearing and shouting in physiotherapy and disrupting the sessions for the other patients. Behaviour modification was our approach and, thanks to Nadina Lincoln, many of the staff were pretty good at reinforcing appropriate behaviour and ignoring inappropriate behaviour, although other patients might not be so good and would shout out "shut up" or "go to hell" to the disruptive patient. Mostly, however, we dealt with these problems through reinforcing, gradually increasing amounts of time without swearing and shouting. If the patients could manage two minutes to start with, we would see if they could manage three minutes, then four and so forth. Rewards might be the opportunity to read a motor cycle magazine for a few minutes, or an extra telephone call home, or perhaps the opportunity to do nothing, which was just what many of the patients wanted.

Although RRC was a centre for adults, occasionally we took in a teenager if there was nowhere else deemed appropriate. One referral was a 13-year-old who had been knocked off her bicycle and sustained spinal injury and a severe traumatic brain injury. Her right hemisphere was particularly damaged, causing visual perceptual and visual spatial problems. Because of her age a teacher came in every day to provide tuition and I remember the teacher saying to me that the girl had a good brain! Well, I knew she had a damaged brain, having sustained considerable damage to the right hemisphere, and verbally she was good as her left hemisphere was unimpaired. This is what caused the teacher to say she had a good brain and me to say she had a damaged brain. At the beginning, however, the major problem was the fact that the teenager swore and screamed so much that her physiotherapy sessions were being disrupted. The physiotherapist working with her realised the girl was frightened and in pain but she had to have the PT in order to stop contractures and to enable her parents to take her out in the family car. I was asked to help stop the swearing and screaming. The girl's parents were mortified, thinking we would assume they had not brought their daughter up properly. They were reassured that we knew it was the brain injury causing the bad behaviour and not their poor parenting. We used a token system whereby the girl could earn a wooden bead if she managed to go for so long without swearing and screaming. These were kept on a string around her neck making a necklace. When sufficient beads were collected, the girl was allowed to exchange her beads for goodies of her choice. These included an extra shopping trip into town with her parents, or a new piece of jewellery. The programme was so successful that we made a videotape of her rehabilitation to show at a conference in London.

Another common problem seen with many of the stroke patients who had sustained a stroke to the right half of their brain causing left hemiplegia or hemiparesis, was unilateral spatial neglect (USN). This is where people fail to respond, report or orient to stimuli on the left-hand side of space. In severe cases, men may only shave or women only make up one side of their face. It is a serious problem, with a poor prognosis if it persists. People with USN typically have accidents, they may trap their hand in the wheelchair spokes or burn themselves on a radiator because they are unaware of their hand in space. Another problem often seen in right hemisphere stroke patients with a left hemiplegia is that they show a flat emotional expression. This is because the right hemisphere is responsible for judging and expressing emotion. Thus damage to this hemisphere may mean people are poor at judging and expressing emotion. This, in turn, can be seen as depression because of misinterpretation of the flat expression. This happened once when we had a young psychiatrist on placement with us at the RRC. He said at ward round that one of the patients was very depressed, to which several of the therapists groaned and said "she's not depressed, she's *leftish*", meaning she was typical of patients with a left hemiplegia. Of course, some patients will have USN and depression. There are a number of treatments for USN (see Wilson, 1999 for the treatment provided for an RRC patient and Tunnard and Wilson, 2014 for several treatments tried for a Raphael Hospital patient).

I became best known at this time for my work on memory problems and began to run memory groups at RRC. Most patients had some of their treatment in groups and I was encouraged to provide some of the group treatments. The way these groups ran is described in Wilson and Moffat (1984). I was also seeing individual patients with severe memory difficulties. My first publication on memory was a RRC man who had survived a brain tumour and had great difficulty remembering people's names. As I was always trying to evaluate any treatment I provided, I set this treatment up as a single case experimental design (SCED: a multiple baseline across behaviours design) and managed to get the resulting paper published (Wilson, 1981). I believe this was the first SCED to be published in cognitive rehabilitation.

A study of another patient with a pure amnesic syndrome was also published in 1982 but before publication I presented the case at a conference where I first met Alan Baddeley, very well known in memory research. I had read his work as an undergraduate and as a graduate. After my presentation he came to congratulate me and I thought to myself I hope he isn't going to expect me to be in awe of him because I am not going to kowtow to famous people. Of course Alan would never expect that and was far more gracious than I was at that first meeting. We met again at another conference a year later when I was less prickly. I told him about a new test I was developing and he became interested in that. He was also keen to see some of the patients at RRC and so began a working relationship that lasted for several years, resulting in a number of publications combining clinical and theoretical approaches.

The new test I was developing was the Rivermead Behavioural Memory Test. This came about because of the RRC therapists. When I started at the centre, I would do my usual neuropsychological assessments and report back at ward rounds saying something like "Mr X is below the first percentile on this particular test" or "Mrs Y is two standard deviations below the mean on such and such a test." The therapists would grumble and say, "But can she go home?" or "Can he return to work?" I did not know the answers to their questions but thought we should be able to use our psychological knowledge to come up with a test more able to provide sensible information for the therapists' needs. So I set out to develop an ecologically valid test, that is to say one that would predict real life functioning. I devised a series of subtests similar to real life tasks such as remembering to deliver a message, knowing where one had left one's belongings, and remembering an appointment. Some of the tasks were developed from work completed at the Medical Research Council (MRC) in Cambridge by Alan Sunderland, John Harris and Alan Baddeley. That is why Alan was interested when I talked to him about my new test and asked if he could collaborate. I agreed but was a little concerned because I thought people might think it was his idea behind the test, given he was so famous. In fact for years afterwards whenever people said, "Do you still work with Alan Baddeley?" I replied jokingly, "No, he works with me." To be fair, Alan never said he was responsible, it was other people who sometimes thought he provided the ideas behind the test. I also taught Alan about SCEDs, which he was unfamiliar with at that time when he was chairing an MRC committee visiting rehabilitation centres around the United Kingdom. Another person on the committee told him not to bother to visit RRC as nothing was happening there! How wrong this person was, as Alan realised and communicated to me later.

There was a momentous happening at about this time, involving Mick who was just about to take early retirement (at the age of 50 years). Alan Baddeley, Janet Cockburn (second and third authors of the *Rivermead Behavioural Memory Test* (RBMT)) and myself (first author), and Mick were talking in a pub about the imminent publication of the RBMT and we were moaning about the length of time from submission to publication plus the miniscule royalties a quite famous publisher was going to offer us three authors. Between us, 13 person years had gone into developing the test. This included all the research that was necessary to validate the instrument and we felt that a share of 5 per cent of sales was insufficient. As we chatted about this Mick suddenly said, "Why don't we publish it ourselves?" We looked at each other with some amusement but Mick was serious. He said he would look into it and get back to us.

The upshot was that Mick checked on costs and possible sales and things looked good. Our bank informed us that he would have to put our house up for a second mortgage and it would then be possible to fund a first run of the test. Mick had a friend who was a lecturer in Graphic Design at the University of Reading and his initial help was to prove exceptional in costing, design and production. Andrew Boag is remarkably talented and this, plus his knowledge of local printers and manufacturers, was of enormous help. In later years his expertise and profound knowledge was made abundantly clear in working meetings that Mick's company, Thames Valley Test Company (TVTC), had with authors of psychological tests. It was one of Mick's greatest pleasures to chair these meetings between designers, authors and himself as publisher when the group worked on design and manufacture. As an ex teacher of English Mick brought his knowledge of language to the meetings and this served him in good stead when final texts were being proofed. He was captivated by these meetings between himself as publisher, Andrew Boag as designer, and the authors as creators and validators of the psychological tests. This new profession for Mick – just as he was taking early retirement from lecturing at The University of Reading – proved to be a fulfilling occupation in his later years. More of this will be written about later on, when Mick and I joined forces to travel the world, me lecturing and giving workshops on neuropsychological rehabilitation and Mick selling tests he had published under the name of Thames Valley Test Company.

I made my first trip to the United States while working at RRC. I registered to attend a workshop given by Yehuda Ben-Yishay and Leonard Diller in New York. Diller had set up the first programme to call itself "Cognitive Rehabilitation" in 1976. I had been doing similar work since starting RRC in 1979 but did not call it cognitive rehabilitation at that time. I had arranged to stay with an American colleague I had met at another conference. I found my way, by public transport, to her flat and basically looked after myself as she was working and not into being hospitable. The workshop was interesting in a way but I found myself quite critical as the presenters seemed to be against any kind of behavioural psychology. That, of course, was my particular interest and how I had been trained. In fact, the procedures used by both sides were often very similar but the names used were different. Behavioural psychology provides valuable tools for measuring everyday practical problems. It also enables us to implement strategies for reducing these problems and monitoring the rate and extent of any change (Wilson, 1987). All these components were used by Ben-Yishay and Diller despite them believing they were not using behavioural strategies. This is not to say that I am critical of these two men. Both have been hugely influential in rehabilitation and Ben-Yishay has since become a personal friend. I admire Diller too for his ethical views and commitment to brain injury rehabilitation.

Every evening while in New York, I went to whichever museum was open late that night. I believe it was on Thursday evening that the

Metropolitan Museum of Art was open so off I went. I was hungry and decided to buy a hamburger from one of the little stalls open throughout the city. There, at the bottom of the steps to the museum, was a hamburger stall. I was in a hurry so marched straight up to the stall and asked for a hamburger. The man looked at me and said, "Ma'am, this ain't a hamburger stall, this is a commercial!" I looked around and then saw cameras and a model in a fur coat. How could I have missed them? This was a good example of selective attention. At first I felt a fool for not seeing the film set but then realised how funny it was.

Another amusing incident occurred when I returned home. I had to phone a hospital in New York and I always tell the switchboard that I am phoning from England so they do not put me on hold for ages. I phoned the hospital on July 4th, forgetting the significance of this day for the Americans. I said I was phoning from England and could the receptionist put me through to the psychology department. The woman said, "Gee, there's nobody there, it's Independence Day." After a brief pause she added, "Don't you have that over there?" I laughed to myself, thinking she obviously did not know from whom they were celebrating their independence!

During my time at RRC, I was also working towards my PhD. I had registered with the University of London. This was because the IOP where I had completed my clinical training was part of London University and as a graduate I could register and pay no fees. I also realised I had to make my research my clinical work so my thesis was a number of studies under the heading of "Cognitive Rehabilitation After Brain Damage". All the studies were work carried out with individuals and groups at RRC. The new test, the RBMT, was one of the studies. I submitted the PhD towards the end of 1984 and was awarded it early in 1985. I remember the viva in London. My external examiner was Graham Hitch, a fair and good man and co-author with Alan Baddeley of the working memory model, which has always been influential in my professional life. The internal examiner, however, Maria Wyke, irritated me from the start. In my introductory chapter I had described the different areas of the brain involved in memory and she wanted me to say that rehabilitation strategies should be different for those with damage to each of these structures. Rehabilitation does not work that way. We target the everyday problems, not the specific area of the brain that is damaged. What really made me cross though was the discussion about validating the test. To be valid, a test has to measure what it says it measures, in my case everyday memory problems. I used three methods to validate the RBMT but the one I was most proud of, and thought the best validation measure, was to ask the therapists working with the patients to note down the memory failures observed in the sessions for me to correlate with scores on the RBMT. I made a checklist of possible memory failures based on the work of Alan and his colleagues at the MRC and asked each therapist from PT, OT, SALT and psychology to complete this at the end of each session. Eighty patients were observed in this way for between 30 and 50 hours each! This is a huge observational study. Furthermore, the correlation between the number of everyday failures observed by the therapists and the scores on the RBMT was 0.75. This is a very big correlation and one I felt really proved the RBMT was a valid measure of everyday memory problems. Maria Wyke, though, said I could not ask therapists to observe in this way. I asked why not and she said it was because they are not allowed to administer standardised tests. I explained that I was not asking them to administer a standardised test just to observe the patients they were working with. She insisted she was right and I insisted I was right. I thought if I were in a pub with her I would walk out but if I walked out then I would never get my PhD, so I stayed, feeling dismayed that I would not pass. Graham Hitch brought the discussion to an end and asked me to wait outside while the two examiners debated the outcome. I went outside sure I had failed. I was invited back in for Graham Hitch to congratulate me on doing such clinically useful work! I could not believe what he was saying and, although pleased, the occasion was spoiled by Maria Wyke's arguments and to this day I feel unhappy about my PhD viva. I was to hear about Maria Wyke much later in connection with Augusto Pinochet (of all people!) as we will hear in a later chapter.

My head of department at this time based at the Warneford Hospital was John Hall, a man I liked very much. Once a month I went to departmental meetings attended by all the psychologists in the Oxford region. May Davidson had retired after my interview and before I started work at RRC. Her successor was John Hall, who always approved of me. May had been ill; what started as foot drop turned into motor neurone disease. I met May once more at a social meeting and heard her interviewed on the radio, I think. I remember her saying she was not frightened of death but feared the process of dying. I can certainly relate to that. I think she died about 18 months after the diagnosis of motor neurone disease, in 1982. An award was set up in her name, the May Davidson award for people who have made a significant contribution to clinical psychology within ten years of qualification. John Hall wanted to put me in for this award the first year it was announced but there was another man also deserving of the award, Bernard Kat, and as he would no longer be eligible the following year, he took priority over me and won the first

May Davidson award. I won the second, in 1985. By this time my first book (after the Penguin Families Project) was published and I was contracted to write another based on my PhD for Guilford Press of New York. The first book with Nick Moffat was a book on the clinical management of memory problems (Wilson and Moffat, 1984) and the book for Guilford Press was *Rehabilitation of Memory* (Wilson, 1987). In fact I have established a friendship with Seymour Weingarten of Guilford and also with a person to join that firm later namely Rochelle Serwator. On one of my trips to the United States, Seymour asked if he could meet me for dinner. He flew me from New York to Boston, took me to dinner in a restaurant where Hungarian gypsies played and it was here we discussed the 1987 book. On another occasion, Seymour took me to lunch at a Japanese restaurant and insisted I use chopsticks which, until then, I had never used. Now, I am an expert with chopsticks and thank Seymour for making me learn to use them that lunchtime.

Life was progressing well, I was publishing, attending conferences, treating patients and giving lectures when we realised RRC was in trouble. The health authority wanted to close it to save money. A meeting was called and one of the senior managers said that if a facility was to close there had to be a three-month consultation period but this could be avoided as the health authority would say they were temporarily closing the centre and then after three months they would really close it! Many of the RRC staff were shocked at this and decided to try to reverse the decision. I wrote to everyone I knew in the world and asked if they would write a letter to the Oxfordshire Health Authority to say how important was RRC and that it should be saved. This duly occurred and the authority was surprised at our abundant support but still decided not to change their minds. A date was set for builders to come in and start demolition. A small group of us met to decide our next steps and concluded we had no choice but to occupy the centre; that is to say, we would take over the running of the centre and prevent any builders coming in. I agreed to chair the occupation committee. There were others just as capable but many feared they would lose their jobs if too closely allied to the occupation. I had little fear partly because this is not in my nature and partly because at that time clinical psychologists were in short supply and there were plenty of jobs available. We were all committed to the belief that patient care would not suffer during the occupation: we would allow no alcohol on the premises and do everything legally. Occupation was, at that time anyway, a legal possibility, even though it remained an extremely frightening action to take! We had to inform the police and put up a symbolic rope barrier across the entrance plus a notice saying this was a legal occupation. We also had to have people at the gate at all times. We could not advise everyone in the centre as we knew that not all thought we were doing the right thing, and if the authority was informed we would be prevented from putting up the notice and the rope. We certainly could not tell the consultant as she would prevent it. I had a trainee with me at the time and she helped to write and laminate the notice. I wondered if I should be asking her to do this but reasoned that if she was going to work in the NHS she should learn how to fight for it.

The day came to start the occupation. It was shortly before Christmas and we knew that the consultant would be out for lunch with her secretary, so we decided that was the time to put up the symbolic rope and the notice. The rope and notice were installed, the police were informed; we had a rota of people willing to be at the gate. This included Mick, who did his regular shifts there. The press was informed and gave us good coverage. We had a brazier to keep us warm and to cook the potatoes that local farmers left for us. Many people going past in their cars sounded their horns to show their support. The police were less enthusiastic and, at first, did not recognise the legality of what we were doing. However, we had a lawyer advising the team and he contacted the police to say that if they thought what we were doing was illegal they needed to change their lawyers. The police attitude changed a little but it was clear they did not like what we were doing. Most of the city did seem to approve though, including of course the Oxford students, some of whom organised a Saturday march in support.

We sent a letter to the health authority saying we requested a three month consultation period as was our legal right. Fortunately, a new chief executive had recently been appointed and this was the first major problem he had had to deal with. Not only that but he was sympathetic to our views. It took 18 days before we received a letter from this man saying he agreed to a three-month consultation period. The occupation was called off and life returned to normal. Nobody lost their jobs. And Mick could stop pretending he was Che Guevara! I was congratulated and received offers of other posts. As far as I know, this was the only successful occupation of an NHS facility.

Although pleased with the outcome (and RRC remained where it was for several years), I was beginning to feel burned out. I had been at RRC for nearly six years and wondered if I should move on. Meanwhile, the head of psychology at Charing Cross Hospital decided she wanted me to work there. She came to visit and tried to persuade me to apply for a post there. I did not want to go and said this, so was asked if I would at least go for a visit. I did and saw someone else there whom I knew and did not admire. He was interested in the post and I thought he was not nearly as good as me. I was introduced to one of the senior medical doctors who

Figure 5.1 Victory for the Occupation! Barbara holds aloft the letter conceding to the demands of the occupiers

asked me why I wanted to work at Charing Cross Hospital. I said I did not want to work there! This led to him persuading me of all the benefits I would get if I did accept the job! I would have extra members of staff and be funded for conferences and so forth. What with these offers, the fact that there was someone applying whom I thought was not very good and I was feeling burned out at RRC, I found myself accepting the job.

Mick and I were beginning to enjoy the benefits of dual incomes, and, combined with payments for my workshops and lecture tours in the United States – as well as Mick's sales of TVTC publications whilst over there – we could afford some interesting road trips around the various states, usually tagged on to the end of one of the workshops organised by Northern Speech Services. This was a company that arranged my presentations and acted as a distributor of TVTC's tests. At the end of a workshop we'd hire a car, usually an Oldsmobile open top, and get on the road, sort of Bonnie and Clyde style – without the violence! One memorable trip was down to New Orleans. We were at a conference there but this was made even more attractive because of Mick's interest in New Orleans Jazz. On this particular occasion we were able to combine an extraordinary variety of experiences based on New Orleans' legacies, which included Cajun and Creole cuisine, voodoo, comedy, the writings of Mark Twain, cruises on paddle steamers, the Mississippi river itself, and of course jazz! I'll go through these in the order we experienced them, beginning with our first stay in a hotel in the middle of the French quarter. We arrived there after being in New York where we had bought a quite impressive wooden African Ashanti sculpture of a woman, naked and about two feet high. It had been wrapped in newspaper and when we got to our room we took it out of its wrapping and placed it on a table and then went out in the early evening to wander round the shopping district. On our return we noticed that there had been a turn down by one of the maids and that we had each been left a chocolate on our pillow. We also noticed that the African sculpture had been left two chocolates at her feet! It was then that we remembered that New Orleans has a reputation for being a major centre for voodoo and we pictured in our minds the confrontation there must have been as the unsuspecting maid looked up at the sculpture for the first time!

That evening we thought we'd sample some of the food for which New Orleans is famous. We found a restaurant in the French Quarter and eventually chose jumbalaya and seafood gumbo, having denied ourselves the chance of sampling shrimp and alligator sausage cheese-cake, red beans and rice, po boys selection, crawfish, pralines, Cajun and creole dishes, banana foster, turtle soup and muffulettas. We did well, even though we never found out what muffulettas were!

On our return back to the hotel Mick had this stupid idea of having his photo taken whilst standing by any street sign made famous by having a blues song named after it! I got fed up with this after we had covered Canal Street, Perdido Street, Basin Street, Burgundy Street, Gravier Street, Magnolia Street, Rampart Street, Franklin Street and St Phillip's Street! When writing this I thought I'd look for the photos but they seem to have been lost! We also fitted in a visit to the Jazz Museum in New Orleans with Louis Armstrong's music playing in the background. We loved the museum but were surprised at how quiet it was; we were almost the only visitors. We think the Americans do not appreciate their wonderful musical history as much as they should.

On the next day we were going on a cruise up part of the Mississippi on the legendary "Delta Queen", a paddle steamer that boasted an original calliope, which was rescued from the sunken showboat "Water Queen". As a pleasure cruiser she was currently famous for serving five meals a day! Mick took a copy of *Huckleberry Finn* with him – as though we needed even more atmosphere! I don't think he even got past the first ten pages of what is generally accepted as an American masterpiece! Not because it isn't just that but because he was so taken up with on board activities involving jazz and food! Our particular trip was known as the "Jazz Feste" because we would be stopping on occasions to pick up a new Jazz Band that would play a different kind of genre from the others. We also had a brilliant resident comedian who, when he found out that the boat had two Brits on board (the only Brits in fact), made a point of picking on us for some of his witticisms. For instance, he talked about his first trip to England when he "enjoyed" a meal of cucumber sandwiches. And so the humour went on for some time as Mick and I continued to be the butt of his very funny jokes. We found it touching that the Americans on board came up to us at the end of the evening and apologised for some of the humour – which we had loved anyway! They should have known that the Brits are past masters at self-criticism! One other thing that happened was that Mick won the jazz quiz, beating all the Americans, and was given a New Orleans umbrella for a prize. Mick's victory is perhaps not surprising given that the British, alongside most other nationalities, were far more interested in jazz than the Americans, some of whom had not woken up to the fact that jazz is originally American music that they have given to the world! Actually, since those days there has been growing interest in jazz by Americans, and several TV programmes about early jazz have been shown on American television, thus stimulating much more interest.

The Delta Queen is a beautiful wooden ship which is no longer allowed to carry passengers on cruises such as ours because of an American "Safety at Sea" act. She is now located at Chattanooga, Tennessee to serve as a hotel and restaurant, beginning in April 2009. Delta Queen fans are still working on getting a renewal of exemption from Congress but this seems unlikely. She was actually built in 1924 to 1927 in Dumbarton, Scotland and she was rushed into Navy service after Pearl Harbour as an emergency hospital transport. She is truly beautiful and is regarded as one of America's historic monuments.

On another trip to the United States, we flew from the conference we were attending to Albuquerque, New Mexico and hired a car. We drove to Taos where we stayed in a beautiful adobe inn. A particularly wonderful landscape opened up to us once we left the main road from Taos in New Mexico and made our way to the ranch where D.H. Lawrence and his wife Frieda had lived for several months after being invited to stay there by its owner, Mabel Luhan, who had been mightily impressed by Lawrence's *Sea and Sardinia*. Lawrence has described this place as his "only true home" compared with the scores of places where they had stayed during their world travels. Built on the slopes of the Mountains of the Blood of Christ, Lawrence and Frieda loved their solitary residence set in the rugged and bountiful landscape. Mick and I approached the tiny ranch with trepidation, wondering what we might find there. We had learned that it had been entrusted to the University of New Mexico and that it was let out sometimes to writers and students as a place of peace and quiet, encouraging creativity. In fact the actual residence was empty and closed but we were able to have a good look round the beautiful garden that included Frieda's colourful grave, decorated with messages of tribute to her and her genius husband. After Lawrence's death in the south of France, Frieda eventually lived at the ranch, where she had many years with her new partner. There were many messages of sympathy and support for Lawrence and Frieda and Mick and I spent some time reading them. We left our own message and gift, which was a library ticket from Charing Cross Hospital. We were stunned by the silence of the place and the gentle breeze that caressed us as we thought about Lawrence's absorbing and tempestuous relationship with Frieda, a woman of the twentieth century, one of the very first to be recognised as genuinely independent by later students of marriage. A cousin of the fighter pilot the Red Baron, who was one of Britain's most courageous opponents in the First World War, Frieda enjoyed her independence to the full in her relationship with Lawrence; and Mick and I have often wondered why Lawrence has been so bitterly opposed by later leaders of the twentieth century's Women's movement. Of course Lawrence had his lengthy passages of silliness when he involved himself in trying to invent a new kind of sexual politics – bound to fail in its attempts to attach spirituality to sex, but, putting this to one side, surely Lawrence remains one of the great writers of the English language.

After our visit to the ranch we made our way back to Taos for one more night to learn that the next day would be one of four in the year when the resident Indians hold their special corn dance, so we got up early the next morning to make our way to the stunning Taos pueblo, the biggest and oldest in the United States, to see and hear residents singing and calling greetings to fellow members of the tribe from the rooftops of the pueblo as they prepared for the dance which would take place later that day. The weather was great, the early morning sun was shining red just above the mountains of the Blood of Christ. This whole scene did have a *genuine* touch of spirituality in its best sense!

6   Charing Cross, Southampton and Cambridge

I knew from my first day at Charing Cross Hospital that I had made a mistake in going there. I travelled by public transport to the hospital and became depressed by the dismal surroundings. I then discovered that I did not have a room to work in. The psychology department felt that neurosciences should find a room for me and neurosciences felt I was the responsibility of the psychology department. Temporarily, or so I was told, a space was found for me in a room shared by four other people from various departments and I stayed there for many months. If I needed to make a phone call about a patient, I had to use the phone in the public corridor. Referrals were very different from the way they had been handled at RRC. There we discussed patients at ward round and, if it was felt that I needed to see anyone, we agreed this after a general debate. If I were to carry out a neuropsychological assessment, a particular question would be asked of me such as, "Does this woman have problems transferring because of problems with language, memory or perception?" or, "Does this man have a problem with anxiety or memory or both?" At Charing Cross Hospital, I would receive a curt little note from one of the medical staff saying, "Psychometry please". I hated everything about the new job and now feel that I went into a clinical depression, measured by the fact that I went home every night and cried. There were some likeable colleagues at the hospital but I never fitted in there. After about ten days, I went to a conference in the United States and was so relieved to escape for a while.

I managed to stay in this job for a year. It never seemed to improve. On one occasion after I had been there for about eight months, I was so fed up with not having my own room that I went to one of the managers to complain. She said that *I* should find a solution as it was not her responsibility! I was furious and wanted to leave the job. I didn't, of course. There were so many times I wanted to walk away and nearly left but two things stopped me: first we needed the money and second I knew that an unexplained break from work would not look good on my CV.

The solution came on a train journey. I had agreed to give a talk in Newcastle at the first World Congress of Neurorehabilitation organised by Michael Barnes. On the way up to Newcastle, I met Lindsay McLellan on the train. I had met him a few times before at the Society for Rehabilitation meetings and I liked him. I told him about my unhappiness at Charing Cross and he said a post was coming up at Southampton Medical School, based at Southampton General Hospital, running the Masters in Rehabilitation Studies Course. The man currently in charge of this course, Ron Tebay, was soon to leave. Lindsay suggested I apply for this post.

In due course, I applied for the Southampton post and went for the interview, which was tough. Not only were there six senior people interviewing me but I knew one of the other applicants was a well-known person who really wanted the job. I realised that this interview wasn't a piece of cake and I had to try hard if I wanted the post, which of course I did, being so unhappy at Charing Cross. One of the interviewers asked questions, which I felt were aggressive, certainly confrontational. He appeared to be a supporter of qualitative research whereas I was more into traditional, quantitative research. The questions kept coming about qualitative research and I felt myself becoming angry. I looked at the others around the table and said that I felt under attack. This stopped the hostile questioning. I was offered the job and went to Southampton where I healed my wounds and came out of my depression.

I was not sure what to expect in my new position and had a variety of different therapists attending the MSc in rehabilitation studies course. Most were physiotherapists, occupational and speech therapists but occasionally other therapists were accepted; we had one chiropodist who did well, I seem to remember. Most had had at least two years' experience since qualification, some had interesting careers and several were from other countries. The first year I was there we had three students from Hong Kong, two men and one young woman, Tatia Lee. At that time Tatia was an occupational therapist (OT) but after gaining her MSc she married, went to Canada and retrained as a psychologist. She is now a full professor at the University of Hong Kong and one of the people I really admire. Another of the Hong Kong students, David Man, is also professor at the Hong Kong Polytechnic University and is doing interesting work in rehabilitation. The third person from Hong Kong has disappeared and nobody seems to know what happened to him.

One of my teaching requirements was to run some practical workshops. I had prepared for these before starting the job. One experiment I ran was to show a video clip of the young girl mentioned in the previous chapter. This showed her shouting and swearing at her physiotherapist. The class had to count how many times she swore. Of course, the first time round there were large discrepancies between class members. We discussed how we needed to define swearing and were we going to include screams or not? We discussed the need for training and we discussed event recording, time sampling, interval sampling and duration recording before trying each of these methods. Interval recording was the method obtaining the best agreement among the class members. At the beginning of the exercise, I saw the three Hong Kong students in a huddle conversing in Cantonese. It transpired that the two men were explaining to Tatia what words were swear words in English!

The second practical was about improving recall of health service information. I tape recorded summaries of four health-related problems: visual object agnosia, unilateral visual neglect, challenging behaviours and memory problems. Each summary was presented in one of the following ways: the first used professional terms and jargon; the second used simplified language in which jargon and polysyllabic words were avoided; the third used categorisation (this meant saying words to the effect of, "First I will tell you what is the matter, second I will tell you what is likely to happen and third I will tell you what can be done"); the final method was to combine simplified language with categorisation. There were 150 words in each passage and each contained 10 main points. The order of presentation was counterbalanced. Participants listened to the tape recordings and, after a distractor task, were asked to write down as much as they could remember. The method combining simplification and categorisation resulted in the best recall. I repeated the experiment with other health care professionals who were attending a one-week workshop on research design. In total there were 32 participants of whom 22 were physiotherapists, eight were OTs, one was a psychologist and one was a medical doctor. As before, the combined method was the best for improving recall. I was pleased with this study and hoped it might persuade health care staff that there were better ways to present information to patients and families. I presented a paper on this at a meeting of the SRR (Society for Research into Rehabilitation) and then published it in *Clinical Rehabilitation* (Wilson, 1989).

I supervised several of the students' MSc projects and learned about a number of physiotherapy and OT practices. One project that impressed me was by an OT who wanted to see whether group training, to teach joint protection principles to people with arthritis, was effective. Before the training, the patients went into a group which met once a week for six weeks to learn about joint protection principles; they were videoed making a cup of tea and making a snack. They were videoed doing the same tasks after the joint protection group training. The group taught them such things as turning on a tap or opening a tin of beans in a way as to protect their joints. The video clips were mixed up and, after some training, two assessors were asked to rate the clips according to strict criteria. Thus, if the tap was turned on in the normal way this step would be scored 2; if it was turned on using joint protection principles it would be scored 0 and if the tap was turned on using a mixture of the two styles it would be scored 1. There were numerous steps for the tasks and each step was scored 0, 1 or 2. The raters, of course, did not know which clips were taken before or after the group training so the design methodology was excellent. Unfortunately, there were no significant differences in the joint protection behaviour after the group training. However, the people attending the group were also given a questionnaire to complete as to whether they were using the joint protection principles taught to them. They *thought they were using them*! Lessons to be learned from this study were first, that the group training given to these people was not an effective way to teach them the principles and second, there was a difference between what people thought they did and what they actually did!

Another study I remember from this time was by one of the physiotherapists (PTs) on this course. She was working with children with cerebral palsy who were required to do exercises of pushing on a table. She wanted to know whether they did better when given feedback from a PT or from a computer. This was when computers were becoming more widely available and starting to be used in education and health care services. The computer was set up so that when the children pushed they were given feedback as to whether they were pushing too hard, too soft or at the right strength. The other condition required the PT to give verbal feedback such as, "That's right, keep going, don't push so hard." Unsurprisingly, at least with hindsight, the children did better when given feedback from the computer. I felt I was learning about much wider aspects of rehabilitation than I had been exposed to formerly.

Soon after I started work in Southampton, my first grandchild was born. This was Anna's daughter. Anna had gone to university to study experimental psychology in Brighton, had graduated and was working as a psychology assistant in order to gain experience to obtain a place on a clinical psychology training programme. This duly happened later and Anna is a qualified clinical psychologist who specialises in adult mental health. Her first baby was born, however, while Anna was an assistant. She was married to Paul and they both shared a flat in Brighton with her sister Sarah. My mother was still alive and in a long stay hospital in Hampshire. She came home for the day on Christmas Day, just as Anna went into labour so I could not go down to Brighton to be with Anna. Sarah was with her for the birth and the baby was born on the afternoon of Christmas Day 1987. Sarah caught a taxi back home after leaving Anna in the hospital and told the taxi driver that she had just seen her niece born. The taxi driver asked the baby's name and was told it was Rosie. He said he liked that name as it could be very posh or very common. Sarah and Rosie always had a close bond until Sarah died when Rosie was 12 years old, as we will learn later.

Meanwhile, I was still publishing with Alan Baddeley, the RBMT was now published and I was getting a reputation as a rehabilitation psychologist. I had not forgotten about the views I had when assessing the woman who had sustained an anaesthetic accident and whom I assessed with the Portage scales. In fact I had continued to assess some people while at Charing Cross, encouraging one of the physiotherapists there to register for a PhD to develop more appropriate measures for assessing people with really severe impairments. She, however, had moved on and taken my idea no further. While at Southampton, the idea of setting up a proper study to develop these measures germinated. I thought that if we observed a large group of people as they recovered from a traumatic brain injury (TBI), we could use these observations to devise a measure to monitor recovery. I discussed the proposal with Lindsay McLellan and one of the statisticians working at the hospital, Michael Campbell and, together, we submitted a grant to The Medical Research Council. This was successful and we appointed a research psychologist, a research PT and a research OT to work on the project. This project was eventually to evolve into The Wessex head Injury Matrix (WHIM). The psychologist, Sandra Horn, was a lecturer on the MSc course, the PT, Martin Watson and the OT, Agnes Shiel were both graduates of the MSc course so I knew them all well. Agnes, in fact, turned this work into her PhD and became the senior author of the WHIM. She later came to work with me in Cambridge before being head hunted by the University of Galway where she is now a full professor and head of department.

The plan was to observe 100 people who had sustained a TBI from two hospitals in the area and see which behaviours emerged during their recovery. These behaviours would be used to construct the observational tool. We actually identified 97 patients, of whom 9 died before they could be observed, so 88 patients were included. This was easier said than done. First, we had to find the patients and they might be on any ward in the two hospitals. We then had to convince the consultants on each ward to let us observe: we reassured them that we were not observing their clinical practice but noting which behaviours emerged as the patients recovered. This involved considerable time and effort. We thought at first that we would see people once they had scored 9 or more on the Glasgow Coma Scale (GCS: Teasdale and Jennett, 1974) as this is the rule of thumb (not always correct) which decides whether or not someone is out of a coma. We soon had to stop this as it became apparent that the GCS was often completed incorrectly. We noticed that some patients were always scoring the same on the GCS and we became suspicious. We thought that nurses were simply filling in the previous scores each time. When they were prevented from seeing the previous score, differences appeared. Consequently, we saw every patient we could as soon as possible.

The typical pattern was for a severely brain injured patient to be admitted to the Intensive Care Unit at the Wessex Neurological Centre. Here they would receive good treatment; once medically stable, however, they would be moved to whichever ward had a bed for them. Often this was to an unsuitable ward where the consultant did not want that particular person under his care (it was always a male consultant). The patient might be expected to die and might not therefore receive the appropriate treatment. The speech and language therapist (SALT) who knew about swallowing might not be called in; the right PT might not be provided; the dietician might not be involved and so forth. We saw several potentially avoidable complications develop among the patients. This might be inhalation pneumonia whereby a patient who cannot swallow is fed by mouth and the food goes into the lungs, causing pneumonia. We also saw contractures, mislabelling of behaviour, falls and insufficient calories being administered.

One of the very first patients was a survivor of the Clapham Junction train crash, which occurred in 1988. We were told he had behaviour problems and regularly scratched the nurses. When observed, we saw that the scratching happened immediately prior to the man opening his bladder or bowels. Perhaps he was signalling that he needed the toilet or a bedpan? Whatever the reason, once the staff were made aware of the relationship between the scratching and the toileting it became easier for them to adjust. Similarly, other disruptive behaviours were seen when there was too much stimulation going on around the patient; so ensuring only two people were present, darkening the room and confirming the radio or television sets were not on all the time could calm people down. We found that we could see more behaviours when people were really motivated. One man who had been a motor cycle enthusiast before his severe TBI kept his head looking towards the left so we tried putting motor cycle videos on a monitor placed on his right-hand side. This resulted in the man moving his head to the right. We demonstrated that this behaviour occurred consistently. Another man was very unresponsive until Agnes put some whisky on his lips: he then smacked his lips loudly and appeared to really enjoy the taste. Of course, it is debatable whether or not alcohol should be allowed in a hospital. The funniest example of providing the right motivation happened with Martin, the research PT. He wanted to know if there was any cognition in a man who seemed to show no response at all. Martin held up a £10 note in one hand and a blank piece of paper in the other. He asked the man which paper he would like. The man's hand shot out and took the £10 note. Martin was not expecting this at all and he said something like "Oh, that was just a test, it is my money and I need it back!" The man laughed and gave Martin his £10 note back! So there was indeed cognition present and the man appreciated humour.

We faced some difficult ethical decisions at times, too. There was one man who had been riding pillion on a motor cycle while under the influence of alcohol. There was a crash, the driver was killed and our man sustained a very severe TBI. At first he went to intensive care where he received good treatment and his life was saved. Because of swelling on the brain, he had a craniotomy (where part of the skull is removed to allow the brain to swell). When he was stable, he was sent to a general ward where he was not wanted and was expected to die. He remained there for several months and was in our observational study. He was one of those people not getting the appropriate treatment. He was losing weight and becoming emaciated. There is a misconception sometimes that people who are not fully conscious need fewer calories because they are not doing much. In fact, the reverse is true. Not only may these people thrash around, they may not absorb their nutrition normally. Well Sandra, the research psychologist, lived near the hospital so she would monitor people at weekends as well as during the week. She became concerned at this man's emaciated appearance and went to see the dietician. She said she had a hypothetical question about the number of calories required by a brain injured man who was not fully conscious. The dietician realised the question was not hypothetical at all and asked the man's name and what ward he was on. Sandra told her, the dietician went to the ward, saw the man and wrote in his notes that his calories were to be doubled. The consultant read this and was furious that Sandra had dared to go to the dietician without his knowledge. He was so angry that he crossed out the dietician's recommendation and wrote "halve the original calories"! He was possibly going to change this but Sandra knew that if the calories were halved, the man would die. It was the weekend and Sandra was so concerned she phoned me, as senior grant holder, at home to tell me the story. I said it was a medical decision and I would phone Lindsay as the medical person in our group. I phoned him at home and, at first, he was cross saying that psychologists were always causing trouble. However, he drove to the hospital, went to the ward and wrote in the notes that he hoped euthanasia had been discussed with the man's parents. This was a recognition that the man would die. Then, the consultant relented and the extra calories were supplied. Soon after the man was transferred to the rehabilitation ward where things started to improve for him. We will never know how much better he might have been had all this trouble not happened.

We were very unsure what to do about this consultant; if we did nothing we were condoning bad practice. If we challenged the powerful consultants, we would not complete the study and thus not provide the evidence we needed for change. We talked and talked; should we go to the local press or the local television station? Should we go to the management at the hospital? There seemed to be no clear answer. In the end we decided to finish the study but to feed questions to the relatives and persuade them to ask the staff looking after their loved ones, "Why are you doing this?" or "Why aren't you doing that?" We did not know if that was the right decision but we did complete the study and things did change, a specialist ward was set up for survivors of brain injury, resulting in trained staff who knew what they were doing and who were able to call in the right people when needed.

On a personal note, Mick and I had just about reached a halfway point in our marriage: It was time to take our breath and gather our thoughts! Sarah was married to Gez and Anna to Paul; all four were living in Brighton; and Anna was about to give birth to our granddaughter Rosie. Both our daughters had completed university degrees at the University of Sussex. Matthew was soon to be married to Andrea, a brilliant winemaker who some years later was to be voted the best winemaker in Chile. Before that however Matthew would be settling into his new job in Chile, as a food and wine photographer. But again I am rushing too far ahead and must get back to a place called Titchfield, a beautiful village with an extraordinary history dating back to the seventh century. It has one of the oldest churches in the United Kingdom. We were enjoying life in a house we bought on Titchfield Square. It was very old, dating back to the fifteenth century, built before Columbus sailed to America. All the houses on the square were built in the thirteenth, fourteenth and fifteenth centuries and they would have been standing when Shakespeare visited the Earl of Southampton in his home territory (assuming that this is one of the stories that might be true of the shadowy figure of the greatest writer on earth!).

During my employment at Southampton Mick's publishing company continued to grow, although it was never big enough to have its own office and warehouse, which were in fact rented from private landlords. Thames Valley Test Company (TVTC)'s biggest boost came from

Figure 6.1 Matthew the photographer. (Image credit: Claudia Maturana)

establishing a business arrangement with an American Company known as Northern Speech Services (NSS), owned by Tom McMillan who became a distributor for TVTC's tests in the United States. In fact, I established first contact with NSS, who organised workshops led by me. The arrangement was for me to run three-day workshops in hotels throughout the United States at the rate of about two or three a year, and at which Mick was present as exhibitor and sales manager of TVTC's tests. This was an amazingly profitable and pleasurable arrangement, which enabled Mick and me to hire American open-topped cars to drive round localities once the workshops were over. To give some idea of the extent of these visits, I can say that I have stayed in every US state except one – which is Kansas. Not many US citizens can make such a claim! We loved these trips and got to know many Americans and appreciated the beauty of the American landscapes: mountains, plains, deserts, rivers, canyons and all the fantastic National Parks including Yellowstone in Wyoming, Zion and Bryce Canyon in Utah and Glacier in Montana. No wonder America makes the best road movies in the world! At times in certain southern states we could drive all day long without seeing more than three or four other vehicles!

Once, after our work, we were driving through the Blue Ridge Mountains of Virginia (made famous for us because of the Laurel and Hardy song). Mid-afternoon, we decided we should find somewhere to stay for the night and left the park at a place called Orkney Springs. Having stopped the car I saw a woman who looked like a local. I went up to her and asked if she could recommend a place to stay, preferably with a swimming pool. She inspected us carefully and then said we could stay with her and her husband. She explained that she ran a home for disadvantaged children from Washington DC but they had no children at the moment and they had a swimming pool. We followed her home, which was a beautiful, white and green ex Civil War Hospital; I believe it is listed as one of the historic places of America. We had our own room and access to the pool. We ate dinner with the woman and her husband but they were teetotallers so there was no wine with dinner. That night we sneaked out into town, bought a bottle of wine and sat on our balcony drinking. Mick said he felt like Clark Gable and said I could be Vivien Leigh for the night! It is one of our favourite memories of the United States.

Another favourite memory is our trip to Chadron, Nebraska. Many people say Nebraska is boring but our visit there was definitely not like that. We had driven from the Badlands of South Dakota. Much of the trip was through back roads and meadows full of flowers, bees and butterflies. We arrived in Chadron, which is in the panhandle of Nebraska. Our first visit in the town was to the Chamber of Commerce, which acts like a tourist office. I asked the man there for a recommendation of somewhere to stay with a swimming pool. He said there were some good log cabins just up the road with a swimming pool. I thanked him and just as we were leaving, he said, "By the way, there is a literary festival in town at the moment." We were delighted, booked in to the log cabin, had a swim and spent the next few days listening to readings from works by Jack London, Mark Twain, Paula Gunn Allen and others. It was indeed a memorable trip. Totally unlike Hollywood, the Oscars or buying and selling, and all the better for that! We especially appreciated meeting literary folk, quiet lovers of literature who somehow seem to be drowned out at times by popular culture and the Americans as presented in the mass media.

It was round about this time that we started to go to Paxos for our annual holiday. Paxos is a small island, not more than 20 square kilometres in size, set in the Ionian Sea just 14 kilometres south of Corfu. For us it is a regular holiday home for about a week each year, usually in the early part of September. We fell in love with it on our first visit when we had been married for about ten years. We particularly enjoy it because it is a working island where the Greeks live side by side with tourists and it is often difficult to tell them apart, although there is one small beach used almost exclusively by the Paxoits close by the town centre. In fact there are no large beaches in Paxos filled with hordes of trendy holiday makers and that is another attraction for us. The best way to get to one of many very small beaches –more aptly named coves, sometimes only big enough to take a couple of holiday makers – is to hire a small motor boat to get there. Indeed, a large number of holiday makers make use of these lovely little boats to get round the island to enjoy the gentle east coast and the more rugged west coast with its sometimes sheer cliffs, caves and arches. On one occasion we were in a small boat going round the west coast when we were shocked by a scene in which two men threw another one off a small cliff into the sea. As we neared the scene we were relieved to note that there were many others there, forming some kind of Greek chorus and that we were witnessing the making of a film!

Another time we met the charming Peter Brook, the famous stage and film director who made the trip round the island in an ancient boat controlled by a single oarsman and we presumed he was making his way to the "golden cave" described by Homer. We instantly fell in love with Peter because of his engaging personality, his wonderful smile and twinkling eyes. Obviously a person who threw himself into life with all its possibilities. And you didn't have to be a film star to gain his complete attention!

The interior of the island is really one great big olive grove with many tiny footpaths through the rugged landscape that leads to cliffs, some of which have gentler slopes that lead to secluded coves ideal for private swimming, which we love. At most times there are breaks in the foliage enabling one to see the vast blue sea, great skies and wonderful sunsets. Best of all are the views of Anti Paxos, a much smaller island to the south, which is now almost a complete vineyard that has its own superb, sandy beaches where the holiday makers based in Paxos go for days of sun bathing, swimming and good lunches of fresh fish, and cool wine.

In the first few years Mick and I used to pay a guy to take us to the southern tip of Anti Paxos and leave us there at a beautiful, secluded beach for the whole day, picking us up in the late afternoon. We had the sea, the beach and surrounding rocks and caves to ourselves, spending our time sun and sea bathing and snorkelling. We had another adventure when we had hired a small boat for the day to sail to Anti Paxos. Everything was fine getting there but the weather turned very nasty, the wind blew in heavy gusts and the sea turned rough. Mick and I decided that the waves were too big for us so we hauled our boat up to the top of the beach and went back to Paxos on the much larger ferry boat. When we went back to the boat owner he was extremely angry and told us that it would be possible to have his boat stolen from that beach so he decided to go back there in another boat as it got darker and darker in order to tie the marooned boat to the one he was sailing and make his way back in the pitch black! A very brave man indeed. Mick refused his invitation to accompany him! We once stayed for a week in one of only three villas on Anti Paxos. There were no restaurants open in the evening so we had to bring food from Paxos and cook our own evening meals while watching rats run along the clothes line! We prefer to stay on the main island but Anti Paxos is great for lunch.

In recent years Mick and I stay at the Paxos Club Hotel, which is very quiet and blessed with a lovely large swimming pool where Mick and I are able to do our regular two hours of sun bathing and we both swim a kilometre: Mick, always in a hurry, and I continuing to do my very slow and gentle free style. From the hotel it is a vigorous walk downhill to the very small town and port of Gaios where we have lovely evening meals while enjoying the sights and sounds of the harbour, the coastline, the bustling marina, the darkening sea and the coast of mainland Greece lit up by the slowly fading evening sunshine.

Meanwhile, I was happy in Southampton; originally appointed as a senior lecturer, I was then promoted to reader and told I was on track to become a full professor. I was still going to conferences and travelling around the world and still collaborating and publishing with Alan Baddeley. He was the director of the prestigious Medical Research Council's (MRC) Applied Psychology Unit in Cambridge (later to become the Cognition and Brain Sciences Unit) and was working to develop rehabilitation research. He wanted me to work there and lead the rehabilitation research team. When he discussed this I said I was happy in Southampton and would soon get a professorship but Alan thought that Cambridge was more respected and I would be better there. Mick, meanwhile, was keen to return to his native Suffolk. He had been born and bred in Ipswich and hankered after a return to East Anglia. Alan was successful in persuading the MRC to set up the rehabilitation research group and I felt it was too good a job to turn down so I applied and had to go to London for an interview at MRC head office. After the interview, I was asked to wait while the interview panel debated. I waited for so long that I thought the chair of the panel was going to tell me I had not been appointed. I was appointed, however, and the delay was because they were deciding whether or not to appoint me at the professorship level. The MRC do not give professorships, their equivalent is Senior Scientist Special Appointment. I was not appointed at this level so I was just senior scientist. The special appointment came two or three years later. After three happy years in Southampton, we moved to Suffolk. I had wanted to find a house in

Cambridge but Mick said we would not be able to afford that and should live in Suffolk. In retrospect he was right, Cambridge is not our kind of place being too elitist. We have lived ever since then in Bury St Edmunds, a town I love, and I am very much an East Anglian now. I will say more about my work in Cambridge in the next chapter as this was the time I founded the Oliver Zangwill Centre. Maybe I should report on one interesting event that occurred during my time in Cambridge, namely an incident to do with Augusto Pinochet.

Many people will remember Augusto Pinochet. He was a Chilean general, politician and a former president of Chile. He became president in 1973 when he overthrew the democratically elected government of President Salvador Allende and ended civilian rule. Pinochet was president until 1981 and was guilty of many abuses of human rights. He then became Commander-in-Chief of the Chilean Army until 1998. In October of that year, Pinochet, who was a friend of Margaret Thatcher, was in the UK. The Spanish wanted him extradited because of crimes against humanity in his native Chile. He was arrested in London six days later and held for a year and a half before finally being released by the British government in March 2000. It was claimed that he had dementia, so a neuropsychological assessment was required. The person found to carry out this assessment was Maria Wyke (the same person who was one of my PhD examiners). The reason for this was that Maria Wyke, originally from Mexico, was a native Spanish speaker and could, therefore, assess Pinochet in his own language.

Soon after the assessment I was telephoned by the BBC's *Newsnight*, a political programme that went out in the evenings. I was asked what I thought of the neuropsychological report. I replied that I had not seen it. The person on the telephone proceeded to summarise the report and asked if this meant that Pinochet could understand any charges if he went to court. I said that if the findings were correct, he would be able to understand the charges but might not be able to remember them. I was then asked if I would say that "on the record". I said I would and was then asked to be interviewed for the television programme that evening. Having agreed to that, a car was later sent to drive me to Ipswich where there was a television studio and I did a remote interview about Pinochet's assessment with Jeremy Paxman, the well-known and often intimidating interviewer. Like most psychologists, I tried to sit on the fence a bit, saying something like, "On the one hand this and on the other hand that." However, as assessed by some later reactions, I must have come across as anti-Pinochet, which, of course, I was.

A few days after the interview, I had a letter from Justicia (an organisation of families of the disappeared in South America) asking for a transcript of my interview, to be typed on MRC headed paper. I duly sent this and forgot about the interview for a while. Then, some weeks later, I had a letter from Jack Straw, the Home Secretary at that time, asking if he could have a copy of my letter for the British Library. I said he could but I wanted the letter to be sent in its entirety. I duly sent the letter and, as far as I know, it is still in the British Library somewhere.

That isn't the end of the story, however. My son was sharing a flat in Brighton with a Chilean girl when her older sister, Andrea, who lived in Chile and was a winemaker, came to visit her younger sister. Matt and Andrea were attracted to each other but she had to go back to Chile after a few days. Matt phoned me and said he had met this wonderful girl but she had returned to Chile and he didn't know if he would see her again. I thought that this might lead to a marriage and grandchildren so I said that I had to go to Chile soon and that Matt could come with me. We went in 2002. I was speaking in Buenos Aires, Argentina first, so Andrea flew to Argentina and we all met up in Buenos Aires. We then flew to Santiago de Chile. I gave my talks and it was time to fly home. Before leaving for the airport, Andrea's mother, Panchi, and her grandmother, Estella, invited Matt and me for lunch. We ate in the garden and Estella said she wanted to propose a toast. I thought she was going to toast Matt and Andrea but no, she said she wanted to toast the British people for taking her in and protecting her from Pinochet. I felt a lump in my throat at this unexpected approval of the Brits. Estella later became a translator for the United Nations but she said when she first arrived at Heathrow, she did not know anyone and was crying in the taxi. The taxi driver stopped the car to buy Estella fish and chips to cheer her up. This is the kind of British behaviour I like to hear about. I also learned that Andrea was born in Buenos Aires because Panchi, who was pregnant with Andrea when Allende was overthrown, was also at university at the time. She missed university one day as she had to go for an ante-natal test. While at the hospital, all her classmates were arrested. Panchi only escaped arrest as she was at the hospital. Because of this, Panchi went to Buenos Aires to give birth.

There is even more to the Pinochet story. In 2004, Matt and Andrea married in a winery in Santiago. The wedding ceremony was half in English and half in Spanish. It was a lovely occasion with the Europeans vastly outnumbered by the South Americans who were also much, much better dancers. The Brits, however, gave speeches and they all wore hats so this made up a little for our lack of dancing skills! Well, before the wedding Matt asked me not to mention Pinochet as there were people present who approved of him saying he had built roads and schools and so forth. I promised not to say anything but towards the end of the evening, Panchi came over to me and said she wanted to introduce me to some people. Way over at the edge of the courtyard were three men. They said they wanted to thank me for what I had done for Chile! I could not think what they meant and said that I drank Chilean wine and I had given them my son. Was that what they meant? No, no, no, they said, we heard about you and Pinochet. So that was the story and, by the way, Matt and Andrea produced two lovely boys, Sammy and Max, so I did get the grandchildren I was hoping for. More about these later!

Just before I left Southampton I was at a conference in 1990. Rohays Perry, who was then in charge of journals at Psychology Press, suggested I start a new journal on neuropsychological rehabilitation. We discussed how this might work and I said I would consider it but wanted Ian Robertson to be co-editor with me. Ian agreed and we invited some others to be on the executive editorial board. The long and the short of this is that we started *Neuropsychological Rehabilitation* in 1991 and it has gone from strength to strength ever since. Our citation rate hovers around the 3.00 mark and our publication is one of the most respected of the rehabilitation journals.

Founding the Oliver Zangwill Centre

I began working in Cambridge in October 1990 and once again felt like a fish out of water. I had understood that I would be based at the nearby Addenbrooke's hospital but it was very difficult to get the right space there and the rooms we thought were going to be allocated to the rehabilitation research group were, in the end, given to another department. Meanwhile I had a room in the MRC Applied Psychology Unit (later to become the Cognition and Brain Sciences Unit). It was a very *academic* unit yet I was essentially a *clinician*. My purpose at work was – and still is – to improve the lives of survivors of brain injury. The main purpose of the senior scientists at the MRC unit, it seemed to me, was to develop models of cognitive functioning. I have nothing against the development of models when it is borne in mind that their essential goal is to help people, but when patients seem to be being used solely to assist in the development of a model then I object. While of course there were people at the MRC who understood my position, there seemed to be others who viewed me as a second-class citizen. I remember at the first quinquennial (five year) review, I felt as if I were seen as less important than other senior scientists there because of my clinical interests. I had to give myself confidence by giving myself a talking to. I asked myself, "Who helps more brain injured people?" and "Who would you rather be treated by if you had a brain injury: them or me?" This helped to bolster me up as I knew that my work was valuable too. To be fair, the MRC head office always saw the value in my work and I think I gave them "street credibility". Certainly, I never had any problems with their five year reviews. Nevertheless, I somehow felt uncomfortable when I was at my daily work at the unit in Cambridge. I went to the regular seminars and talks and, wearing my clinician's spectacles, nearly always felt "so what" after the presentations. I was not interested in reaction times or understanding prepositions or the tiny bits of cognition that many of the talks were about. I wanted to know, for example, how to teach people to use a compensatory memory aid or reduce family distress, and these sorts of questions were not part of the domain at the MRC.

Ian Robertson was to join our rehabilitation research team and we were both allowed to appoint a junior research fellow. I knew Ian as we had trained together at the Institute of Psychiatry in London before he moved back to his native Scotland to work in alcohol addiction. He later changed his interests to neuropsychology with some help from me when I had gone to Edinburgh to give him a crash course in neuropsychological rehabilitation. Well, Ian came to Cambridge and I had another ally. I decided I needed a qualified clinical psychologist to be my research fellow and remembered my last trainee at Southampton, who was Jonathan Evans. He had been excellent and I wondered if he would be interested in the post. Jon had now qualified as a clinical psychologist and was travelling around the world before starting work. The problem was how to contact him before the closing date for the applications? I managed to track down Jon's mother who told me Jon had a "post restante" address in Thailand so I wrote there thinking it was a long shot (this was in the days before emails and mobile phones were in common use). The day before the closing date I had a transferred charge call from Thailand! Guessing it was Jon, I agreed to pay for the call. Jon was very apologetic at transferring the charges and said he had tried and tried to pay for the call himself but just could not get through. I told him not to worry and explained about the post. He wanted to apply and I was able to complete an application on his behalf before the interviews in Cambridge, which would take place once he returned home from his travels. Jon returned, he was interviewed and appointed and that was the start of a long and fruitful working relationship.

Ian also appointed a research fellow, we were allowed a secretary for our research group and things started to feel better for me at the MRC. I continued to see patients, my research involved developing new assessment and treatment techniques for people with non-progressive brain injury. I published frequently, and had many invitations to speak and give workshops abroad. These early workshops were in fact the beginning of a huge part of my career that has lasted for several decades and has contributed to my tally of over a hundred countries visited, some of which I hope to describe in the rest of this book.

My first trip to Australia took place in 1992 when the International Neuropsychological Society and the Australian Society for the Study of Brain Impairment (ASSBI later the Australasian SSBI) held a mid-year meeting. Mick and I went, had a great time, fell in love with the people and the country, and I have returned several times since. I have been for some time now an honorary professor at the University of Sydney.

My grandfather was born in Sydney and left there in around 1900 to come to England to find a wife. He married my maternal grandmother who refused to go back to Australia with him and he remained in the UK for the rest of his life, so I missed a chance of being a fully fledged Aussie! I remember in the early days of my London life my grandfather's Australian accent and the red cheeks he always had, that were possibly burned forever in the Australian heat.

Anyway, on my first trip to Australia, ASSBI arranged a conference dinner which included an exhibition of sheep shearing. Edith Kaplan (a well-respected and important American neuropsychologist who sadly died in 2009) managed to grab a pair of shears and pretended to chase a young man around, threatening to cut off his pony tail. That was funny. I was interested in learning how the sheep were sheared and watched one of the shearers very carefully. He was not a talkative man and I tried my best to get him to tell me about his job. It was hard work! Then I asked him what kind of sheep they were. "Suffolk" he said brusquely. "Oh, I live in Suffolk," I said. At that his demeanour changed and he became friendly. "Do you?" he said. "What's it like, is it very green?" I agreed that it was green. "You wouldn't think these sheep would do so well over here would you," he answered. I had finally found the right question to ask him.

On a later trip we had a real scare. In 1995 we were going to a meeting in Australia but had to be in the United States at another meeting first. For this reason, we flew from Los Angeles rather than going from London via Singapore or Bangkok. We were flying directly from LA to Sydney. About halfway through the flight, there was an announcement from the cockpit asking if anyone had lost a radio. We heard a boy in the row behind us say that he had lost a radio. One of the stewards came to talk to him and then said that the boy's radio wasn't the one they had found. Soon after that we had another announcement asking us to pass all our blankets and pillows to the aisle as "we sure do need them". We passed the blankets and pillows and as they were being collected, I asked the stewardess why they were needed. She said that the captain would be giving us an explanation soon. This duly came: we were told that an unexplained device had been found on board and had been moved to the back of the plane. The captain had been in touch with Sydney and as there was nowhere to divert to, we would continue to our final stop. Meanwhile, people at the rear would be moved forward. Some people started praying and some started singing but most, including us, were very quiet.

Mick and I were near the rear of the cabin so we were among those to be moved. As we stood up I looked behind me and saw a huge pile of blankets and pillows. I thought to myself that if the device was a bomb and exploded, the bedding would not have protected us. The stewardess pointed to a seat for me but there was nowhere nearby for Mick so I said to her that if I was going down, I was going down with my husband. She then found us two seats, near one another but not next to each other. Somebody behind us said, "Gee what do you have to do to get into club class?" Part of me imagined arms and legs flying through the air and part of me did not believe this would happen. I wanted to get a message to Sarah telling her to keep the family together if anything should happen to us. We had already been given landing cards so I decided to fill mine in to pass the time. Then I needed the toilet and asked a stewardess if it was OK to go. She said yes, so I went and, as I sat on the toilet, I said to myself "Barbara, what do you think is going to happen?" I then replied to myself saying "Barbara, I think you are going to get out of this."

We approached Sydney and the pilot kept us informed of progress, he told us when the wheels were going down, so we would not be scared by the noise. He also said that we would land at a remote part of the airport and we would be met by the emergency services. He said "We will have an expeditious and orderly exit of this plane." We thought the captain was excellent, keeping everyone calm. We landed safely and saw blue lights of the emergency vehicles waiting for us. We filed off in almost complete silence using both sides of the plane. We were moved to another part of the airport and met by Ms Keating, head of QANTAS airlines and sister of, the then Prime Minister of Australia, Paul Keating. There had never been a scare like this in Australia before. We were told that the bomb squad were going on board to rate the danger from 1 to 4. If it was a 1 we could all go on our way, if it was a 4, however, we would be detained. The bomb squad report came back saying it was a 4! I thought we had been lucky.

At this point, we were all taken to the first class lounge and more details began to emerge. While on board, an 11-year-old girl, travelling with her grandmother, had dropped something under her seat. When she felt around to look for it she found a radio wrapped around with sticky tape and wires sticking out. This was the radio we had been asked about.

Then some of the Americans telephoned home and we learned that the Unabomber (a notorious person responsible for several terrorist attacks in the United States) had placed a letter in the *San Francisco Times* a short time before saying that a device would be placed on a plane leaving Los Angeles within four days. The pilot, of course, knew about this but most of the passengers did not.

Eventually, the next report from the bomb squad arrived saying that no explosives had been detected on the device, it had been made to look like a bomb but it wasn't a bomb. We never found out just how this device had been smuggled aboard. We were told that if we wanted to go, we could and our luggage would be sent on but if we wanted to stay and collect our luggage then that was fine too. As Mick and I were staying in Sydney that night, we decided to wait for our luggage. It came at last and we left the airport feeling high having survived this scare. At the exit were several reporters checking the luggage labels. They saw ours and asked if we were willing to talk to the press. We were only too ready to talk to anyone, having come through a potentially fatal situation. We spoke to the press and were to find ourselves on the front page of the *Australian* (one of the national newspapers) the next day.

Meanwhile we took a taxi to our hotel, The Old Park Royal on the Rocks, to check in. At the check-in desk, I told the receptionist that we had been on the plane with the bomb. She said "Well that deserves an upgrade," so we were upgraded to a good room with a great view of the Sydney Opera House. We went out for lunch on the waterfront and had rather too much alcohol because we felt so high and then spent too much money on new clothes.

The next day we flew to Cairns with Ansett, the Australian Domestic Airline (this no longer exists) where we were to catch a ferry to Hayman Island and the rehabilitation meeting. We told the Ansett staff that we had been on that plane with the bomb the day before so the Ansett staff gave us a bottle of wine! We caught the ferry to Hayman Island and went to the welcome reception. As we were rather late, we were among the last to arrive and when we walked in a huge cheer went up. Many people had seen our photograph on the front page of the *Australian* so treated us as heroes. The next day, the manager of the Hayman Island resort told us that at that moment we were his most famous guests. A short time before, Tony Blair had met Rupert Murdoch on Hayman Island to discuss Murdoch's support for the Labour Party in the next general election. Tony Blair won this election in 1997.

Another place in the Great Barrier Reef we loved was Heron Island, a coral cay, shaped like an unshelled peanut. Although very small, it packs a considerable punch for holiday makers. It is situated near the tropic of

Capricorn at the southern end of the Great Barrier Reef. Despite being only 800 metres long and 300 metres at its widest point, its seas contain 900 of the 1,500 fish species found on the Great Barrier Reef, and 72 per cent of the coral species growing there. Its dunes and forest supply a habitat for thousands of nesting birds at different times in the year. The island has a resort that can host 200 guests and a research station run by the University of Queensland. The two run happily and quietly together, the scientists pursuing their research and the holiday makers participating in snorkelling and scuba diving. The pure white beaches are never crowded and one appreciates the beautiful seascapes. There is always a guide to introduce paddlers and less adventurous swimmers to the flora and fauna of the shallow waters. It's easy to get there from Brisbane, either two hours by boat or less than an hour by plane.

Mick and I have visited Heron Island on two occasions, separated by many years. The first time we were there was when we were with a group of delegates from an international conference, members of the International Neuropsychological Society. We stayed for three days, I think, and I remember how impressed we all were with the weather, the beautiful beaches and crystal clear sea. It seemed like paradise! Mick remembers one evening when they had a fashion show attended by several tall and elegant models from the mainland who had to change rapidly on several occasions in a big wooden shack with only one large window with no curtains or shutters. It wasn't long before several male members of the group appeared in the dark by the space in front of the window to obviously talk seriously about psychological matters. They learned that the models either appeared to have the briefest of underwear or nothing at all to go under the costumes they were due to show after they all scuttled to get changed as quickly as possible into those costumes before walking elegantly in front of potential customers who remained oblivious as to the hustle and bustle that had gone on backstage!

Other travels during this time included a trip to the Galapagos Islands with Mick, a trip to Jordan with Sarah and a trip to Madagascar on my own although I joined a group when there. These were all holidays and were with Explore Worldwide, which I called "middle-class roughing". Mick found travel difficult at this time because he had developed arthritis in his right knee. This was because of football, which he had played well into his fifties. When the doctor diagnosed the condition he told Mick it was his age, to which Mick replied that the left knee was just as old as the right and that knee didn't have any problems! Consequently, I started travelling without Mick but then he had an artificial knee fitted and became active once more. It felt magical to have this new knee fitted.

Before the Madagascar trip Sarah introduced me to the gym where she went several times a week. I knew there would be trekking in Madagascar and I would be one of the oldest people if not *the* oldest person on the trek. I did not want to make a fool of myself so Sarah persuaded me to join the gym. I did and still go several times a week to this day! I think I'm pretty fit for my age. I was the oldest person on the trip to Madagascar and even started "the old ladies club" for the four or five oldest women there. I had improved my swimming too before the Galapagos trip. I taught myself to swim at Camberwell Baths when I was 11. When I knew we were going to the Galapagos Islands I realised it would be possible to swim with sea lions so decided to learn free style (front crawl) with my head properly down in the water when breathing out. Mick was an ASA swimming instructor so, with his help, I learned to swim properly and still enjoy swimming a kilometre once a week when home and every day when on holiday. I can swim easily now, I have plenty of stamina but I'm very slow! Oh, and I did get to swim with the sea lions in the Galapagos Islands.

7 Founding the Oliver Zangwill Centre

One of my work trips was a three-month sabbatical in Phoenix, Arizona at George Prigatano's unit. I wanted to see how his programme worked so arranged to go in 1993. Sarah and Anna were both married then, Sarah had married Gez and Anna had married Paul. Rosie was nearly 4 years old. Anna and Paul were soon to separate and then divorce. Sarah and Gez were very involved in mountain biking and edited a somewhat scurrilous fanzine. I went to Phoenix and rented a hospital flat, which I didn't much like, and frequently spent the night at a hotel.

The work at the hospital was interesting. I was impressed by Pamela Klonoff, one of the senior clinicians at Prigatano's unit and also by one of the occupational therapists (OTs) there, Sue Kime. It was while observing Pamela Klonoff one day that I thought her work and style with the patients was clinically excellent and the kind of rehabilitation I would want for my nearest and dearest should they ever need such a thing. I saw an amnesic patient with Sue Kime too and we discussed a programme for her. Sue bought a sophisticated organiser that I thought was far too difficult for such a severely memory impaired patient but I was proved wrong. Sue taught the young woman how to use this organiser, helped by one of the psychology fellows working there at the time, David Lamb. The study was written up and published (Kime, Lamb and Wilson, 1996). Despite this and other successes I was very lonely and missed my family. Sarah and Gez were visiting San Francisco while I was in Phoenix so we arranged to meet up for a weekend. I remember meeting them at the airport and clinging on to Sarah, so very pleased to be with someone I loved. Mick also came out for a few days, so that helped too. I knew he would hate the hospital flat so we stayed in a hotel while he was there. Phoenix is the fifth largest city in the United States and the largest in Arizona, a beautiful state, the home of The Grand Canyon, which I have visited on two occasions. One beautiful city in the State is Sedona and another much smaller city is Tucson. To my mind, other places in Arizona are so much more interesting than Phoenix. Tucson, for example, the second largest city in Arizona and home to the University of Arizona, is surrounded by the Sonora Desert with the wonderful saguaro cactus. I much preferred Tucson. In fact my friend and colleague Elizabeth (Betty) Glisky lives there. Later Betty and I went on a cruise to Fiji together in between conferences in Hawaii and New Zealand. I mention this briefly in Chapter 9 when I discuss my training for the London marathon.

I felt I had learned from my experience in Phoenix and went home with ideas buzzing around my head. Soon afterwards I was at a brain injury meeting in my home town of Bury St Edmunds and met Tony Jewell, a community physician whom I liked. I was telling him about my recent trip to the United States and said that was the kind of rehabilitation centre where I wanted to work but I did not want to move to the United States. Tony told me that I should put in a business case to the local health authority. I thought that would not come to anything but I should try it anyway. In April 1993 negotiations began with the local National Health Service Trust. A business case was prepared and submitted to the local Health Authority who discussed this and asked for further details. Some senior people provided support, including The Medical Research Council (MRC). Although the MRC is not allowed to support clinical work, it does support research and, as my employer, it was prepared to support the Centre as part of my research programme. Other senior people within the Health Authority also provided support. At the same time there were others who did not want the Centre to succeed partly because it was to be sited in a small country hospital rather than the main teaching hospital in Cambridge and partly because there would not be a medical doctor in charge. There were five main reasons why I did not want a doctor in charge. First, I felt that a doctor would insist on being the boss and would not be democratic. Second, our patients would not need medical care even though they would need, at times, access to people who were medically qualified. Third, a doctor would not understand the long-term educational aspects of the kind of rehabilitation I wanted: long-term rehabilitation requires re-education rather than medical supervision. We wanted all decisions to be democratic and inter-disciplinary, something that was felt to be easier if a non-medical person was the team leader. Fourth, a doctor would be too expensive and fifth we wanted our centre to be based on Prigatano's, which was run by a psychologist.

The reason for being located away from the big university teaching hospital in Cambridge was space. The country hospital could provide adequate facilities and car parking for families while, at the main hospital, it was difficult to access these facilities. In addition the atmosphere at the country hospital was calmer and more conducive to the needs of the patients.

With a few false starts and setbacks, it took three years to get permission for the centre to go ahead. I had to choose a name for it. I wanted to call it after someone British, someone who had pioneered brain injury rehabilitation, someone dead (so as not to offend anyone) and someone with a pleasant sounding name. I chose Oliver Zangwill, sometimes called the father of British neuropsychology. Oliver was born in 1913 into an interesting and distinguished family that had emigrated to London from Riga, Latvia in the 1860s. Oliver's father, Israel Zangwill, was a novelist and playwright who wrote both comedies and tragedies about the ghettoes. One of his murder mysteries was made into a silent film. A street in the East End of London is called Zangwill Road after Oliver's father. Oliver's grandmother was one of the first women doctors to practise in England although she had to study in France because women were not allowed to study medicine in England at that time. Her thesis was examined by Paul Broca. Gregory (2001) reports that Oliver's first recorded experiment took place when he was 8 years old. He knew a woman who claimed that she could always tell when rats were present. Oliver hid a rat under his collar and then kissed the woman who did not detect that anything was wrong!

In 1932 Oliver went to Cambridge University to study Natural Sciences and in 1935 graduated with a starred first degree. From 1954 until 1984 Oliver was to be professor of Psychology at the University of Cambridge but before that he went to work at Bangour Hospital, Edinburgh helping soldiers wounded in World War Two. He told Richard Gregory, an old friend, that this was the most creative period of his life. It was during this period that Oliver became one of the pioneers of brain injury rehabilitation. His papers are still worth reading today. I had to obtain permission from MRC head office, the University of Cambridge and Oliver's widow, Shirley Zangwill to use this name. They all agreed and Shirley said that Oliver would have been tickled to know a rehabilitation centre was to be named after him.

We appointed the first member of staff in July 1996, we arranged for three months of staff training and planning the programmes before admitting our first clients. One of the main staff trainers was Sue Kime, the OT I admired in Phoenix. She came over for a few weeks to train us. The centre officially opened in November 1996. Most of the patients who have attended over the years are funded by their own local health authorities with the remainder being funded by Personal Injury Lawyers and compensation claims. The few private patients are those from overseas and we take these reluctantly as rehabilitation is concerned with helping people return to their own most appropriate environments and it is difficult to reintegrate people to their own environments from far away.

I spent two and a half days a week in Cambridge and two and a half days in Ely at the Oliver Zangwill Centre (OZC) where I was director of research. Jonathan Evans was our first clinical manager until he was head hunted by Tom Macmillan in Glasgow in 2006. Jon moved to Glasgow where he is Professor and runs a post qualification training course in Neuropsychological Rehabilitation. He remains there to this day. From the time the centre opened the main problem encountered was obtaining funding from local health authorities. Many of these authorities felt that rehabilitation was too expensive and so were reluctant to fund the OZC programme. Given that most of our patients are young people who have survived an acquired brain injury and will, on the whole, live a normal lifespan, they deserve to be given every chance to live as normal a life as possible. There is evidence to show that rehabilitation may be expensive in the short term but it is cost effective in the long term (Prigatano and Pliskin, 2002). Funding issues initially became easier once the centre was up and running for a few years but it has once again become more difficult, not just for us but in general (Worthington, da Silva Ramos and Oddy, 2017). It remains our main cause of difficulty.

Personally, until the year 2000, things remained good. In 1994, the Encephalitis Support Group began. This was later to become the Encephalitis Society. I saw my first patient with encephalitis in 1979 when I started work at Rivermead Rehabilitation Centre in Oxford. There was no encephalitis society at that time. I was perfectly able to carry out a neuropsychological assessment and help the team plan a rehabilitation programme but there was no support for families. Through my work I knew only too well the devastating effects of this illness on families and individuals. In 1994 I heard about the support group from Elaine Dowell and began to meet Elaine at meetings. Elaine Dowell is the founder member of The Encephalitis Society. For many years she was the main spokesperson for this society and she has seen it grow from a small group of parents of children who survived this illness to a flourishing society encompassing parents, spouses, neurologists, neuropsychologists, psychiatrists, occupational therapists, speech and language therapists and, of course people who have survived encephalitis. In addition, The Encephalitis Society now holds its own conferences, produces literature to help families and professionals and funds research. Ava Easton joined the society in 2000 and became chief executive officer in 2011. She has shown passion and flair in her pursuit of the aims of the society. I became president of the Society in 2007 and remain so at the time of writing. Without Elaine and, since her retirement, Ava's tireless and passionate commitment, it is unlikely that this society would have survived or grown to its present level. In my own field of brain injury rehabilitation, the patients most frequently referred for cognitive rehabilitation are those with traumatic brain injury but after that the diagnostic group most seen are survivors of encephalitis. Before the society was established in 1994, there was almost nowhere for families to go for information, advice and support. Now, it is the first port of call for families and also in many cases for professionals. Initially Elaine and more recently Ava have played a very large part in setting up the society, ensuring its progress over the years, seeing it through the transition from support group to a society and bringing together survivors, families and professionals.

My second granddaughter, Francesca, was born while I was working at the Oliver Zangwill Centre. She was born in March 1996. This time I was able to be present at her birth. Anna and Rosie were living in Bury St Edmunds then, so were Sarah and Gez. Francesca's father was an art teacher Anna had known for many years but they were never married. He died when Francesca was at primary school. In March 1996, Anna went into labour and was taken to the West Suffolk Hospital in Bury St Edmunds. I went too. The labour was straightforward; each time Anna had a contraction, I said to her that she now had one less contraction to face. I reminded her of all the blue cheese she could eat now – and the champagne she could drink. The midwife must have realised I was sensible and asked if I wanted to help. Of course I did. The midwife told Anna that she wanted this baby born soon. I helped the baby out and was the first person to speak to her. I welcomed her to the world and said she had a very nice family waiting to meet her. I then cut the cord under the midwife's instructions. I had always wanted to be a midwife and that was the closest I have ever come. The next day Sarah, Rosie and I went in to see Anna and Francesca. It felt very primeval with the three generations of women together.

The worst moment of my professional career also happened while I was working in Cambridge and at a meeting of The British Neuropsychological Society (BNS) in London. Together with Narinder Kapur, I had founded the BNS in 1989. Earlier, Narinder had approached me and Alan Baddeley to discuss the possibility of setting up the new society. The idea was to bring together the clinical neuropsychologists from the Neuropsychological Interest Group, cognitive neuropsychologists from the Cognitive Neuropsychology Interest Group and those interested in localisation and other neuropsychological issues. We wanted a society that would bring together the different interests in neuropsychology. I became chair of the steering committee and Narinder was secretary. We persuaded Elizabeth Warrington to join the committee, which also included

Alan Baddeley, Michael Kopelman, Karalyn Patterson, Elaine Funnell, Andrew Mayes and Jo Willison. With the BNS formed, Elizabeth Warrington became our first president. The first BNS meeting in the Wolfson lecture theatre at the National Hospital was a sell-out, with people sitting on the stairs! I was president from 1996–1998.

To get to the moment which was so painful for me. One year Karalyn Patterson, a good friend, was organising a symposium at a BNS meeting on semantic memory impairments and asked me to give a talk on semantic memory problems in people with acquired brain injury. I talked about four patients – two with a traumatic brain injury (TBI) and two with encephalitis. My argument was that two of the patients had problems with the semantic memory store and two with access to the store. Replication was the key to answering this question. With repetition those with access problems could sometimes answer semantic questions and sometimes they could not; whereas those with a storage problem could never answer. I thought I did a reasonable job of my presentation but one of the people in the audience stood up to ask a question. He said when you did the replication did you use the classic "blah blah" (I have forgotten the term) method or the less classic "blah blah" method? At first I thought he was joking and I laughed saying I had simply repeated everything. Then he proceeded to tear me to pieces, metaphorically speaking. I was appalled and didn't know what to say. One of my colleagues later called it "gratuitous academic violence", and another said the questioner hadn't done himself any favours. They did not say this, however, until after the event. I managed not to cry in public but spent many an hour sobbing after that. Why was this man so nasty to me? Was it because he felt I was encroaching on his territory or because he thought I needed taking down a peg or two? I don't know. It wasn't so bad that the people who knew me well had seen me so humiliated, it was the students and more junior people I felt should not have seen me in this situation. My son's friend, a PhD student from Brighton, had come especially to hear me. I had known him since he was 2 years old and he saw me being so embarrassed. I felt horrible about that. The following year, in a quiet road in Angers in France where Mick and I had both been at a conference, the man came up to me and apologised. I told him it was fine (even though it wasn't) but I thought to myself why was his apology given so privately when his humiliation of me was so public? I still feel bad about that but after Sarah's death, which we will hear about in the next chapter, it was no longer important.

I won several awards for my work, including an OBE from the Queen in 1998. Sarah had put me in for this and persuaded families of patients I had worked with to write in support. I came home from one of my overseas work trips in October 1997 to find a letter from the Prime Minister, Tony Blair, saying he had it in mind to recommend me for an OBE for services to medical rehabilitation. If he did this, would I accept? I sent the letter of acceptance off with some doubts. I was not a fan of royalty and knew that if I received the award, I would have to go to Buckingham Palace. On the other hand, Mick was thrilled and said it would be really good for rehabilitation if I accepted. The letter said not to say anything to anyone and, in any case, I wasn't sure if this meant I really would receive the award so I kept quiet. Sarah and I were in Jordan for New Year in 1998 but we phoned home to wish everyone Happy New Year and learned from Mick that I had indeed received an OBE in the Queen's New Year's Honour's list. He had been interviewed by local television as I was not available. Sarah and I were in Wadi Rum in Jordan, we told the others in the group and had an impromptu party in the desert that night.

We had a choice of dates for the actual investiture and I chose to go in May. Each person was allowed to take three guests so I went with Mick, Sarah and Rosie who was then 10 years old. We stayed the night before in the Savoy hotel, having driven there in Mick's semi sports Mazda car. The following morning we told the Savoy staff that we were going to Buckingham Palace and were advised to walk there but we had a parking permit and wanted to drive through the gates. We had an interesting day. Prince Charles was giving the awards that day and we were told that was good because the Queen gave each person 15 seconds whereas Charles gave everyone 30 seconds. The guests were led to one room and the people receiving awards were given a lesson by the Prince's equerry, a tall man, who had to show the females how to curtsey! We were told to walk in one way, curtsey and walk forward. When the Prince shook our hand that was the signal to leave and we should back out before departing in the opposite direction. I waited in a queue between a woman getting an award for services to marriage counselling and another receiving an award for services to the National Trust. I liked the awards because they were not academic but given for public service. It seemed a good thing to me.

When it was my turn to speak to Charles, he said to me, "So you come from that famous place?" I didn't know if he meant Cambridge or The Oliver Zangwill Centre or what so I said, I work in Cambridge with people who have survived a brain injury. He asked if we had made any progress to which I said yes, but we needed more money. "Oh, the perennial problem," said the Prince and put out his hand – my signal to go. I don't think I should have mentioned money! I am not sure how much the OBE has helped rehabilitation but some people are impressed with me having an OBE. It stands for Order of the British Empire and, of course, we no longer have an empire so it sounds a misnomer. Sometimes I get letters addressed to Professor Obe!

One last memory before I come to Sarah's death is the millennium, New Year's Eve 1999/New Year's Day 2000. As a family we had a long discussion about where to go for the millennium. We seriously considered Australia: Mick and I had been to Tasmania the year before and discovered Wineglass Bay, one of the most beautiful places in the world. We actually asked the owner of the nearby lodge if it would be possible to book several rooms for the millennium but were told the whole lodge had been booked for that occasion. We considered Heron Island in Northern Queensland, another area we love, but we then learned that the box jelly fish are around at that time and it isn't possible to swim in the sea. We changed countries then and decided to go to Mauritius instead. We went and that turned out to be our last family holiday with Sarah. There were good things about Mauritius, including an interesting submarine trip and a place where Matthew learned to water ski, but we also had a number of family rows – as our family tends to do anyway. The story I want to relate, however, happened just after we arrived. We were met by a minibus from our hotel near Grand Baie and we all piled in. Just as I sat down I was stung on my arm. It was a very painful sting by, I now believe, a hornet. I thought it would get better and for several days tried Anthisan, an insect bite soothing cream we had with us. That didn't help. I saw the hotel staff who told me to continue with the cream. By now my arm had swelled and was very hard and bumpy. It felt like a cheese grater. Eventually, Sarah, Anna, Matthew and Mick decided I had to go into town and see a pharmacist. We all went by taxi and I went into the chemist's. The pharmacist who did not speak English took one look at my arm, rushed around the counter, took hold of me and led me to a nearby doctor. The doctor, who spoke English, gave me some antibiotics and explained that my arm would not have improved on its own. She also said that if you get stung under water you need to put something as hot as possible on the wound whereas if you get stung on land it should be as cold as possible. Well I was treated for the hornet sting and it gradually improved over the next few days. We stayed awake to see in the new millennium and arrived home safely.

8 The death of Sarah, journey to the Cotahuasi Valley, finding The Compassionate Friends and the importance of family

This next section is taken from the book Mick and I wrote about coping with Sarah's death (Wilson and Wilson, 2004) with permission from Wiley.

Monday, May 15th, 2000. It was nearly 3.00 in the afternoon. I wanted to leave work early as my granddaughter, Rosie, had an orthodontist appointment at 4.30 in Bury St Edmunds. I was going to look after Rosie's little sister, Francesca, while my daughter, Anna, took Rosie to have a brace fitted on her teeth. My son, Matthew, was in Philadelphia and my older daughter, Sarah, was in Peru on a white-water rafting trip. Rosie and I were due to meet Sarah in Peru for a 10-day holiday later in the month.

I went into the next room to my colleague, Agnes, and said, "I'm leaving soon because of Rosie's orthodontist appointment." Agnes replied, "No you can't because Mick's on his way to meet you." My husband, Mick, had told me he had to go to Cambridge railway station that afternoon to meet an American visitor who was coming for a meeting with Mick and other publishing colleagues the following day. I said to Agnes, "No, Mick's not coming to see me, he's coming to Cambridge to meet an American guy at the station." Agnes said, "Well he phoned Eve." Eve was another colleague of ours. "What would he phone Eve for?" I said. Agnes would not say – she was being cagey, so I went to Eve's room and said, "Did Mick 'phone you?" "Yes," "Why?", a vague noncommittal response came – "He's coming over, can't you wait for him?" I felt myself getting cross. I wanted to be home and look after Francesca and start the cooking. I phoned Mick's mobile number and was put through to the messaging service. I said, "Mick, I'm not waiting for you in Cambridge, I'll see you at home tonight." I locked up my room and went to leave but Agnes came out to stop me.

"Barbara, you can't go, there is a real problem and Mick is on his way to see you," said Agnes. "It's not Sarah and that bloody rafting?"

I answered. She gave me a strange look – in retrospect I knew she was saying, "Yes", but I didn't want to understand that so I said, "Maybe it's my cat, maybe my son-in-law has run over the cat." In my head I said, "Please let it be the cat, please let it be the cat." I love my cat Django but I knew I could live with his death. Never for a moment did I think "Matthew (our son) has been shot in Philadelphia," even though "Philly" is a dangerous city with lots of guns.

The next thing that happened was another colleague, Tom, came in and said, "Mick's on the phone – on my extension – and he sounds in a state." "Why doesn't Mick ring my extension?" I thought. I went into Tom's room and picked up the phone. Mick had heard my message and wanted to stop me leaving. He was crying and said, "Barbara, there's terrible, terrible news." I went cold and calm and said, "Is it Sarah?" "Yes," replied Mick. "Is she dead?" I asked. "We think so," said Mick, "she's missing and was last seen floating face down." "Well that's it," I replied. "I can't wait to see you," said Mick. I put the phone down and looked at Tom who said, "She's only missing." I was furious and said, "Tom, I'm not a fool." I went to Agnes and hugged her then paced up and down until Mick arrived. We saw him at the barrier to the car park outside our offices. I gave Tom my car-parking ticket and he ran down to Mick so he could get through and park.

I met Mick outside and we hugged each other crying together. He came in while I saw Agnes to tell her what parts of my schedule to cancel. I was quite calm and controlled then. There were meetings for the rest of the week and a talk I was giving for the Leonard Cheshire Homes up north on Friday. My secretary, Julia, was on leave that Monday but Agnes said she'd deal with everything. We left Mick's car in the car park and took my car home. On the way, Mick told me the story from his side.

He had been at work early that afternoon when his colleague, Denise, answered the phone. She said to Mick, "There's a Max Milligan for you." Mick's knees buckled. He knew there must be something wrong in Peru as there would be no other reason for Max Milligan to phone. Indeed we had only heard the name a few days earlier when Sarah had called from Cusco in Peru. She told us that she had met a guy called Max Milligan and had been on a mountain bike ride with him. Then this call. Mick took the phone and Max told him that there had been a terrible accident and Sarah was missing. He said he would give Mick a few minutes and would telephone again five minutes later. He did phone back and we learned that there were two rafts each with five people and a local guide. Sarah was on the first raft. The raft had been stuck in a "hole", a hydraulic (I always see this in my mind as a whirlpool). The raft upended and all five fell out. The guide was able to remain on the raft. Four people were saved and Sarah was last seen floating face down. She had died on the Friday – May 12th – they had searched for two days but her body had not been found. At this stage we just heard the bare details. Mick telephoned our son in America and told him. He did not tell Anna as he thought she was at work and he wanted to tell me himself. He telephoned Eve to tell her to make sure I waited for him to arrive.

Sarah, Matthew and Anna were very close. There was less than 3 years in age between them and all of us kept in touch every 2 or 3 days, if not sooner. I had had an e-mail from Sarah on May 7th saying she would not be in touch for 12 days because she'd be in the wilds. I e-mailed her on the 7th saying "take care with the rafting", and again on the 11th to await her return. Matthew, thinking that Anna knew the awful news, telephoned her. She was really pleased to hear from him and then realised he was crying. She thought something had happened to him. When he told her about Sarah she kept saying, "Not my Sarah, not my Sarah," over and over. Matthew then wondered whether he had dreamt Mick's phone call.

On the way home from Cambridge we telephoned Anna and arranged for her and the two girls, Rosie and Francesca, to come to our house. We arrived home, shocked and weepy, although fewer tears flowed then than later. "Isn't it terrible?" I said to Anna, Anna was sobbing. Rosie, my granddaughter had always been close to Sarah, in fact Sarah had been present at Rosie's birth on Christmas Day 1987, over 12 years earlier. For the following days Rosie was always drawing pictures of Sarah and copying photographs of her. Francesca, who was four, was also attached to her auntie but she did not cry so much. She asked questions like – "We'll never see Sarah again will we?" We did not feel, however, that Francesca understood the finality of Sarah's death. None of us probably did at that stage.

My next job was to telephone my sister-in-law, Carol, who lived near Ipswich, about 25 minutes' drive away. Carol is my best friend and one of the strengths of the family. Carol and her husband Peter were out but I left a message saying Sarah was missing, probably dead and to phone us.

Mick and I decided we had to get Matthew home as soon as possible. I telephoned Matt in Philadelphia and said I would try to get him a flight that night. By now it was about 6 pm in the UK and 1 pm in Philadelphia. I then called British Airways and said, "There has been an unexpected death in the family and I need to get my son home from Philadelphia to London this evening if possible." The British Airways staff member I spoke to was great. She said there was a seat available that evening for £106 (a very low price – was that because of the circumstances, I wonder? I will never know). She also said that Matthew would have to go to the ticket office in Philly and give a reference number and that she would tell the people in the office there what had happened so they would be kind to Matt. Such kindness from her and from the other good people at that time will not be forgotten. It meant so much to us then to know there were good people around. I phoned Matt to tell him what to do. He cried copiously. We were all crying frequently but I felt I had to sort things out as best I could, so I kept in control as much as possible.

Carol and Peter had, by now, heard the message and called to say they were on their way over. They arrived and Carol cooked something for us. I don't remember the details of the evening but we talked and talked and cried and cried. I remember feeling shocked at some point in the evening that I felt hungry. "How can you be hungry?" I said to myself, "when your daughter has died?" But I was. I didn't eat much but I ate something.

Perhaps it was surprising that we did not hope that she would be found. At times I did, there were moments that day and the next when I thought that she might be washed up and found by some villagers. "Perhaps she'll be found with amnesia," I thought, "and they are trying to establish who she is." I always knew though that this was wishful thinking. The fact that she had been last seen face down, unconscious, and that the rafters had been searching for three days, told me that she was dead. Somehow we got through the evening. Anna, Rosie and Francesca went home, so did Carol and Peter, and eventually Mick and I went to bed.

We hardly slept. I managed an hour and Mick probably had the same. I felt so tired and wanted to sleep, but as soon as I came close, I jolted awake with the horror of it all. Eventually I slept but jolted awake again after an hour thinking, "Please let it not be true". Then the ghastly realisation that it was true. I said to Mick, "I need a cuddle." He obliged, we were both needing physical contact and held each other frequently in those early days.

One thing that made me feel particularly terrible was remembering the previous weekend. On Friday May 12th, the day Sarah died, I was giving a one-day workshop in Belgium. I came home that evening and got ready to go to Brighton the next day to attend a memorial service for Alan Parkin, a colleague who had died unexpectedly of a heart attack the previous November at the age of 49. I was, of course, totally unaware anything was amiss with Sarah. On Saturday May 13th, Mick and I drove down to Sussex University for the service. It was a beautiful sunny day and I was somewhat regretful that I could not sunbathe in the garden. During the afternoon I saw Alan Parkin's elderly mother crying. I said to another colleague, Narinder Kapur, who was sitting next to me, "How terrible to outlive your children." Narinder said, "It's the worst thing." We stayed in Brighton that night and I went to a dinner with Alan's

Figure 8.1 Sarah was a keen skateboarder who once skated for England

friends and colleagues. The next day we drove home after breakfast. During the drive I said to Mick, "Life is good at the moment. Work is going well. The kids are all sorted and we don't have to worry about money." Sarah was already dead and I had no idea! If there is any spiritual communication or life after death, or any of those things, then I would have known she was dead or would at least have had some sense of foreboding. She was my firstborn, most wanted, most treasured, most beloved daughter and I'd lost her. I always told her I couldn't live without her, she knew how much she was loved by her parents, her sister and her brother and she left us in such turmoil and despair.

I went back to work after three weeks but it took a year before I could work a whole day and six months before I had my first day without any crying. I thought of Sarah all the time, in the car, in the gym, in the swimming pool, when I was cooking, when I was washing up, it was non-stop and totally exhausting. I was so tired, I fell asleep frequently. I changed from being unable to sleep to sleeping all the time. I even began to sleep at work for a few minutes at a time. I would put my head on my desk and doze off. This was so unlike me as I am known for my energy. I have always been passionate about my work but now it all seemed so meaningless. I went in each day but spent most of the time crying. I couldn't face seeing patients or going to meetings. The most I could do was the post, reading the odd report or thesis and a bit of writing. I was so slow and inefficient that I felt I shouldn't be paid. Mick was also in a bad way. Anna and her brother Matthew were also suffering. Matthew and Sarah had many friends in common and shared similar tastes in music. He always felt able to talk to her and rely on her to help sort out his problems. Anna was very depressed, Sarah was her best friend, her main babysitter and close confidante. All three were born within three years of each other and were very close. In fact we almost always saw each other every day and if we couldn't meet we were on the telephone all the time.

In the bereavement book (Wilson and Wilson, 2004) we tell about the early days, the helpful and less helpful comments made by various people, the attempts to find out how to get a death certificate and our first trip to Peru with Anna, Matthew and Rosie. Francesca was not allowed to come because she was too young to go to such high altitudes where she could have died. At this time we discovered The Compassionate Friends (TCF), a support group for bereaved parents, grandparents and siblings. I learned of TCF through my colleague Ian Robertson, who had worked with me in Cambridge before moving to Trinity College Dublin. Five weeks after Sarah's death, Ian telephoned me to tell me to contact a solicitor called Graham Peart who was the secretary of TCF. Ian said they helped people who had lost children, including adult children. I tried to get hold of Graham Peart on Friday afternoon. He was out but his secretary said he would telephone me on Monday. This was the first time I had ever heard of The Compassionate Friends – a group that we came to admire considerably. Graham Peart phoned. He listened while I told my very tearful story. Then he told me that his daughter had also drowned. She was 4 years old and had drowned in a school swimming lesson. It was so sad. Everything was so very hard to bear. Graham Peart told us that The Compassionate Friends Society was having a weekend gathering in Leicestershire in July. He said there would be about 200 people there and many would have been bereaved in the past year. He said he took six months off work when his daughter died. I had only taken three weeks so did not feel so bad about leaving early and taking the odd day off. I certainly did not feel guilty. I thought "nobody can say anything to me when I've been through this awful tragedy". There were calm periods and by mid-June the calm periods were probably getting longer but the bad periods would suddenly re-emerge with a vengeance and then everything was as bad as it had ever been – like a kick from a horse or an iron rod thumping one in the chest.

I booked, by telephone, two places for Mick and me at The Compassionate Friends weekend in Leicestershire for the coming weekend. I was not at all sure that it was the right thing to do. I felt I was "clutching at straws" and prepared to do anything that might ease our immense pain. Friday July 7th was the day we went to the weekend meeting of TCF. We were both nervous. We knew it would be emotionally draining and we did not know how we would get on with the other bereaved parents. Although calmer, the tears hit us suddenly and unexpectedly. They also stopped quickly. It was a strange sensation, not like ordinary crying which subsides gradually. This grief-stricken crying would be fierce, sudden and then stop without a slowing down period. Matt also seemed a little calmer during his daily calls from the States. Anna was low. She was quiet more than tearful and very supportive to me. She was always willing to listen. I was very glad to have Anna around so much but I knew I should have had two daughters not one. The family seemed so shrunken. I wished I'd had more children when I was younger. I should have had six, not three. I looked at mothers and daughters in the street and thought, "I hope their daughters grow up safely."

At mid-afternoon Mick and I set off to drive to Bosworth Hall at Market Bosworth on the Leicestershire/Warwickshire border. We arrived just after 5 pm, went to the registration desk in great trepidation and were greeted by one of the "old hands", Dinah Perkins. She looked at us and said, "Is this your first time?" I burst into tears and said, "Yes, our daughter died eight weeks ago." "Eight weeks!" she answered in shock, "you come with me." She arranged for someone to take our bags to our room, explained a few things to us and saw to our registration. She was good and kind and we were just so overcome with sadness and grief. The next thing we went to was a "Newcomers Group". We did not like it, we felt uncomfortable, the group leader was not particularly competent in our eyes. There was one couple we liked, from Teesside, but we felt most people were emotionally crippled. We said to each other that we did not want to be like them, we would cope, we would be different, we would be whole. We then joined others to go to a dedication for a rose garden. We did not think much of that either – it was too religious for our tastes. We knew that The Compassionate Friends was not a purely religious group – it was for all religions and for those without religion. Nevertheless, the dedication was religious.

Dinner was at 8.00 and we were invited to join the table of the woman who had led the Newcomers Group. We were not very comfortable, although we met a woman from Suffolk, Eileen, who was the only other Suffolk person there. She had lost her only son Oliver in a car accident in 1993. She had also had a stillborn son years before and she was a widow. I said to Anna, when we had first heard about Sarah, "I could have been a widow with an only child," and now I had met one. We also met an English couple, David and Janet, living in Belgium. They had lost a daughter, Eleanor, from cancer in 1998. As Mick and I were going to be in Belgium the following week for a conference, we arranged to meet up with them for dinner in Brussels. We drank too much wine, did not sleep well and woke up Saturday morning feeling very low. We decided we would leave after breakfast.

Dinah Perkins came up to us at breakfast to find out how we were. We said we were thinking of leaving. She said, "Why don't you go to the keynote speech? Sit near the back in case you need to leave, but give it a try." We thought we might as well do that.

The keynote speech was the beginning of our commitment to The Compassionate Friends. The speaker was a nun – Sister Frances Dominican. She had started "Helen House" – the first hospice for children – in Oxford in 1980. She said she would not mention the "G" word, which made us laugh. She told us about Helen – the girl Helen House was named after and who is still alive but comatose. She told us how she started to help Helen's parents and then took the very sick little girl into her own cell at the convent to give the parents time with their other child and each other. This was a woman who did things. She set up the hospice and several others have followed since then. I thought "this is a really good person". Sister Frances Dominican was a delight to listen to. I felt so pleased to know there were good people around and privileged that I had been able to listen to her.

After coffee we went to a workshop called "Sudden Death". There were several workshops going on simultaneously and each attendee chose which to attend – or not to attend any if they felt like it. We were not sure how the workshops were organised but typically there are about 12 people or so in each workshop; the leader introduces himself or herself and then each person in the groups says who they are, where they come from and a few words about their son or daughter. Then the discussions start and may go in several directions. We thought the "Sudden Death" workshop was good despite being full of heartbreaking stories. We heard about children dying in pain, dying after long drawn-out illnesses, being murdered, committing suicide. We kept thinking, "At least our Sarah did not die in pain, she was happy up to the end – well almost to the end as we don't know about the last few minutes. At least she was enjoying her final hours." We learned fairly early on though that each bereaved family seems to need to find people worse off than themselves, so for us it was, "At least she didn't die over a long period in pain." Those whose children had died in such a manner said to us, "At least we have a body." People kept telling us how brave and strong we were to go to such a meeting after only eight weeks. We were not brave and strong, we were just normal people trying to cope and find something to ease our pain and take us through this passage of grief.

We found ourselves drawn to many of the people at the workshop. There was a woman called Margaret whose daughter Kirstie died eight years ago aged 17½ of a pulmonary embolism. Another woman called Angela had lost her 6½-year-old daughter, Megan, of a brain haemorrhage. Then there was Betty whose 19-year-old son died in a climbing accident. She said, "If he wasn't taking risks he wasn't happy." That sounds like Sarah, I thought. The saddest story to me was of Natalie, a 13-year-old who had died in agony, surviving for 26 hours with gangrene of her internal organs following chemotherapy for leukaemia. The couple from Teesside, whom we met and liked the night before, were there. Their son, Philip, was killed in a car accident 18 months before. They were still very raw and fairly recently bereaved. We were by far and away the most newly bereaved, however, and also the most tearful.

After lunch we joined a tour to the Bosworth Field battleground where Richard III lost his crown to Henry VII in 1485. We talked to several people about their losses and their children. There is an immediate bond between bereaved parents that crosses all walks of life and social class. Mick spent a while talking to a man whose son had committed suicide. Mick seemed very affected by this story. We felt the parents whose children had committed suicide may have had a harder cross to bear. When we got back to the room Mick rested and I went for a swim.

Dinner was better. We joined a table full of people we found it easy to get on with, including the two leaders from the Sudden Death workshop, Sheila and Peter Clarke, and the Pringles who were the main organisers of the weekend. After dinner we decided to go to a session called "The Power of Music" where participants can play a piece of music that means something to them or to their dead children. We had taken Bob Dylan's "Forever Young" but it was on CD and the tape recorder could not play CDs. Most of the songs played were too sentimental for our tastes but a couple were good and moving. One father played a piece composed by his deceased daughter.

The following morning we went to a session on poetry and prose that we particularly enjoyed. Trish and David Lloyd ran it and chose some excellent pieces, most of which they read themselves. Mick read the Wordsworth poem we had selected for the memorial invitations and a few other people read things. One piece Trish and David Lloyd chose and read was from A. S. Byatt's "The July Ghost". I had not known this before and was much affected by it. A. S. Byatt had lost a son herself when he was 8 years old, I believe. One of the reasons why this story touched me so much was that the author becomes concerned with grammar. She hears her husband say about their son, "He is dead" and she thinks "is dead, is dead", this present tense will always be the present however long her son is dead. She also chides herself for being concerned with grammar at such a time. I was intrigued as Mick and I had recently had a discussion about grammar. He wanted to say in the invitations to the memorial service that Sarah would love you to come but was worried that made it sound as if she was alive. I told him that it was OK to say that and he said "Yes, death overcomes grammar." It made me aware that after death one is tripped up by grammar. We frequently spoke of Sarah in the present tense, "Sarah loves potatoes" or "Sarah enjoys that kind of music." We gradually changed "Sarah *loves* to *loved* that" and "Sarah *enjoys to would have enjoyed* that." Even today though we are likely to talk about Sarah in the present tense. Sometimes for a split second I forget about her death. I might think "I wonder if Sarah will phone today." Once the thought has crossed my mind, I remember immediately that she has gone and gone forever.

Everyone we met at the Gathering was kind to us and all recognised how early it was for us. There was one phrase we heard though, that caused us distress. This was, "The second year is worse than the first." That could not be true, nothing could be worse than our grief in those early months. I was clinging on to the hope and belief that in a year's time this awful pain and despair would have subsided, at least a little. One woman who said it so tritely had no idea what a blow this was to the newly bereaved. The couple from Teesside who were 18 months down the line, and still wracked with grief, recognised our dismay and were able to say to us that the second year was not worse.

After the coffee break Mick wanted to read the paper. I wanted to go to another workshop. He checked out, then sat in the lobby reading. I went to another session called "Does grief ever end?" This was run by Iris and Joe Lawley, co-founders of The Compassionate Friends. Even though they lost their son 30 years earlier, Joe Lawley shed some tears in the workshop. I was awed by this. Thirty years after his son's death and he still cried. I thought this was another good workshop and I realised that only the Newcomers Group on the first evening had not worked for us. It was a very sad and emotional occasion but two things were said that I clung on to and remember regularly. Iris Lawley said at one point, "Instead of an open wound, grief becomes a scar." Angela, the woman who had lost her little girl aged 6½ also said, "My life now is full and meaningful." I needed to hear that. A woman from Northern Ireland, Anne McGamingle looked after me, regularly passing tissues and being supportive.

I met up with Mick for lunch and we talked to Freda and Max Bonner who had lost a son aged 28 of a rare form of cancer. He was a Buddhist. We also spoke to a couple from the Netherlands, Jan and Betsy, whose daughter had been killed in a diving accident in Kuwait. Like us, they felt they had to go to the place where their daughter had died, in their case Kuwait, and be as close as they could to the place where she was last alive. We also met a woman whose son had died in a motorcycle accident in Peru. She felt differently from us though. She had never been to Peru, did not want to go and did not like Peru. She hated hearing the word "Lima" in the phonetic alphabet. In contrast, we felt tied to the country, loved it and its people and were sure we would go back.

The closing ceremony was from 2.30–3.30 pm. This was another occasion where we wept a great deal – particularly me. We made our goodbyes to various people and left at 3.55 pm. I was shattered and fell asleep within ten minutes of leaving. We arrived home just before 6 pm and then went round to see Anna who was well but sad. We had not spoken to Matt for several days.

On reflection I felt the weekend was well worth going to, despite being so emotionally draining. We were all in the same club. A club none of us wanted to join and yet we needed to meet people who knew how we felt. There were four main sources from where I found succour. First was that there were so many worse deaths than Sarah's. Although the loss was as bad as anyone's, the manner of death was not as bad, it would have been worse to know she had died in pain or awful circumstances. In the national news at this time was the little 8-year-old girl, Sarah Payne. She was missing. We all knew she must have been murdered even though her parents were hoping she would be found alive. She was later found dead. That was a much worse death. The second thing that helped was to have met so many good people. I wanted everything and everyone to be good. There should be no more pain and sorrow in the world. Our pain was huge and sufficient for the rest of time. Mick, Anna, Matthew and I all felt we had become better people, more tolerant, less worried about trivia. At the same time we had not been bad people before Sarah's death and would have preferred to stay as we were. The third thing I took away from the weekend was that people do manage their grief better over time. Nobody was as tearful and distraught as we were, even though tears flowed freely from many people. I could see there was a possibility of living some kind of life not constantly wracked by pain, despair and agony. Finally, Iris Lawley's comment that "the open wound becomes a scar" helped me through. I wanted to be in a time when the wound would start to scar over.

We continued with life and, of course, there is no real choice but to go on. To this day in 2019 we frequently talk about Sarah and refuse to make death a taboo subject, but we wanted to make a trip to where she had died to make a final goodbye a year after she died. We had been to the river where she died a week after her death but we could not get to the actual spot. Mick and I managed to do this the following year. In our bereavement book we call this the final goodbye and this is part of that chapter (Wilson and Wilson, 2004).

The Final Goodbye – Peru May/June 2001

We left Los Angeles on Friday May 25th and went first to Dallas. I phoned Anna from the airport. She was well. Rosie was in France on a water sports holiday (she promised us she would not go white water rafting). Francesca spoke to me and said she had a dream about a lady in Peru (this was probably her old dream about a lady going in the river). It was hard to understand her though, she was shouting and this distorted the sound. We landed in Lima at 11.26 pm but did not get to our hotel until almost 1 am. Paul Cripps had arranged for a local company to meet us and the driver was elsewhere so we had to wait.

The following morning we were met by a driver from the company, taken to the airport and caught the plane to Arequipa. We took off at 11 am and landed at 12 noon. Arequipa is a beautiful location. There are stunning, white-topped mountains all around. Pepé Lopez was there to meet us. We found it easy to relate to him. He seemed straight and honest, and his English was good. We went to La Hosteria, the pretty hotel we stayed in last year where the woman held me and remembered Sarah. She was still working there. Pepé talked to us for a while about the trip and then left us for the afternoon. After unpacking, we went into the city centre, had a good lunch and then sat in the Plaza d'Armas watching people and pigeons. It is (or was) a picturesque square (just after we returned home we heard about a bad earthquake that damaged the city centre of Arequipa).

Back at the hotel we sat on the terrace taking photographs and video film of the views surrounding us, before resting in the room and then changing to meet Pepé for dinner. We went to a good restaurant, one we had been to last year, with a condor tethered in the garden. To see the condor there is sad. Pepé talked about the next few days. I said "We want the truth even if it is painful." He said he would tell us the truth. I mentioned that we had heard slightly different versions of Sarah's last minutes and were hoping Pepé could provide the definitive version. He thought the different versions were due to the fact that people had seen the accident from different perspectives. Earlier that day Pepé said he had followed Sarah down the river for about 20 minutes. This worried Mick who thought she might have been struggling in terror and pain for that time. I thought it meant that Pepé had followed her body for 20 minutes. In any case, we would hear on the trip or at the accident site.

On Sunday May 27th, we left Arequipa in a minibus at 6.30 am. We had a driver called Edwin and a cook called Raoul. Edwin and Raoul did not speak English. Raoul turned out to be a very good cook. He had worked for tourist trekking companies for a few years. The journey, mostly on dirt roads, to Cotahuasi town was pretty awful. We thought it was even worse than last year. Pepé said they had had more rain in the rainy season this year. The scenery near Arequipa was harsh and barren with no vegetation at all in some areas. The occasional fertile valleys were pleasant enough and, as we pushed on, the scenery became more beautiful and dramatic. The snow-capped peaks with their brilliant blue backgrounds are lovely. Because of the altitude, it was cold. At 8.30 there was a brief stop for petrol and toilets and another stop at 10.50 in a pretty town called Chuquibamba. Here everyone was out in their Sunday best. There was a festive atmosphere because of a children's band playing in the square.

The next stop was at 1.45 for a welcome picnic lunch prepared by Raoul. We pushed on and the road, at times, was truly atrocious with pot holes and narrow paths overlooking steep drops. As we neared Cotahuasi town we had to reverse for over a mile because a bus was coming from the town and there was only room for one vehicle at a time on the road. Since leaving Arequipa we had seen hardly any traffic. The area was very remote, empty, beautiful and dangerous. Pepé showed us a photocopied journal article about the first people to kayak down the River Cotahuasi. The article was frightening as it showed how dangerous the river was even for experienced people – and Sarah was not experienced. Mick said that if Sarah had seen the report she would not have gone on the trip. I was not so sure as she was foolish about her sporting activities. (We include the article in the book.)

I slept for several hours on and off in the van, perhaps because of the altitude. For much of the time we were travelling at around 5,000 metres (i.e., 16,400 feet). We arrived at the hostel in Cotahuasi town exactly 12 hours after leaving Arequipa. This was the same hostel the five of us stayed in last year, with the flooded courtyard. There was no flooding this time. The owner remembered us and was friendly and welcoming. The food was better than last year because Raoul cooked it. We slept well.

The weather on the following day was glorious, bright, crisp and clear showing the magnificent mountains nearby at their best. While

Pepé, Edwin and Raoul were loading the van, Mick and I set off for a quick walk around the town, which still seemed in a time warp. We filmed the blacksmith shoeing a horse (a good scene), but we also saw a little girl, possibly aged about eight years, who was looking after two drunken or drugged parents (not a good scene). Earlier, Mick had seen the man lying with his back against a wall, with his hat pulled down over his eyes – "Looking like a scene out of a Clint Eastwood film." Mick ran back to get his camera but when he returned the man was rolling in the road in torment, his wife was on the pavement in a stupor, and the little girl was trying to get her father to sit up. She looked at Mick with embarrassment as she vainly pulled at her father's sleeve. Mick turned away in respect for the little girl. Later we were to talk about this incident and Mick compared the wonderfully happy but short life of Sarah with what must be going on in the little girl's life. We knew that Sarah had had an almost idyllic childhood in comparison and wondered what lay in store for the little girl.

At 10.10 everything was ready and we set off to collect the mules and donkeys at a lower level in the valley. We reached there at 10.45. There was a considerable amount of unloading of the van and loading of the pack animals, so Mick and I went off for a walk. Pepé had hired a father and son to look after the animals. There were three donkeys, which carried most of the luggage, tents and provisions plus two mules which carried a few things and one horse who did not carry anything (the load distribution did not seem fair to me). At first we followed the same track that we had taken last year. By 1 pm we were near the Sipia falls, close to the place where we held last year's ceremony. We did not feel the need to go to the falls again so pushed on. We stopped under a tree for a snack and to wait for the others to catch up.

The next part of the track (part of an old Inca trail) was steep so Pepé suggested we ride. I was given the horse and Mick one of the mules. After 20 minutes Mick said he wanted to walk as he did not feel in control. I was enjoying the ride and felt the horse was probably more sure-footed than me on the steep, shale-like, path. Mick is always more nervous of animals than me. He said he was petrified! He walked the rest of the way while I did a mixture of walking and riding. I had to dismount for the steep downhill parts and rode going uphill. Eventually, however, I just walked as I needed to stretch my legs.

The scenery was spectacular with wonderful mountains, colours and shapes. I found it extraordinarily beautiful, the most beautiful scenery I had ever seen. I know Sarah would have loved it and I was glad she had experienced such beauty before she died. On the other hand, neither she nor I would have known about this place if she had not gone on the trip and, of course, I would prefer never to have seen this beauty if it meant having Sarah back. We reached Chaupo, our camping spot, at 3.50 pm. It was an oasis of green in the rocky surroundings. The place was a farm and Sarah had stayed there too on her way to the rafting part of the trip.

Raoul prepared us a salad of apples, raisins, chicken and cheese. The animals had a good drink in a stream and Pepé talked about the accident. He said that Sarah was conscious at first, and had looked directly at him from the water as it swept her past him. She was the last of the five to come out of the "hole". The raft had not turned over as we had thought but had upended, so the guide had remained on the raft. We had always wondered why he did not go in the water too. So five people went in the water and Sarah was the last to emerge from this whirlpool-type place. Pepé thought she might have broken her neck just as we were told at the memorial service. At first she was choking and in the correct position but soon after there was another rapid. When she emerged from that she was completely lifeless and just tossed about. Pepé followed her by boat, and on foot, for about 20 minutes but she was floating very very quickly. It was so, so sad. My poor, lovely, beautiful girl. I wanted her back so very much.

We walked to the tents that had been pitched in a field owned by the farmer. Again, it was so beautiful there with the steep mountains, the lush meadow, the tethered pack animals and the farmer's cows and dogs. Our animals had a good feed from the tall grass around. Earlier in the day we had seen a herd of llamas. They looked as if they had been dyed as their coats were a mixture of rust and white. However, Pepé told us these were old Inca colours and quite natural. We had seen lots of llamas grazing over the past two days, but this morning's group were being herded. We had also seen an eagle and several hawks but very few people and no tourists of course. Raoul provided a good meal that we ate under the stars. We had soup, beef curry and rice together with a bottle of Chilean wine. We went to bed surrounded by the tethered donkeys, mules, horses, cows and sheep.

On May 29th, we enjoyed a breakfast of hot French toast (Raoul managed a different hot breakfast each day). Our "showers" were pretty basic, we were given a basin of water each just like my trip to Mali a few years before (Michael Palin was in Mali at the same time making a programme and once stayed in the same hostel as us. I met him briefly in the toilets!). We trudged across the field to find a toilet spot and became covered in burrs so spent ages de-burring ourselves. I was not completely successful and kept finding burrs for days afterwards. Some even turned up back in England. Pepé, Mick and I left at

8.30. I found a stick that helped me up and down the steep parts of the trail. Some of the paths were tricky being shingle and shale on precipitous cliffs and narrow paths so we had to go very slowly in some places. After three hours we stopped for a snack. Each morning Raoul gave us a bag with fruit, chocolate, biscuits, a granola bar and a soft drink to keep us going between meals. All the mineral water was provided too. We never finished our snacks but it was good to know we had these emergency rations.

At noon we moved on again and first saw the accident site from above. Pepé told us that two donkeys had been stolen from the trip with Sarah, and that one of these had been carrying all the safety gear so the group had to wait two days for replacement safety gear. He said that if the gear had arrived one day later, the whole trip would have been aborted. That made us feel very bad. Just one more day and they would never have started that wretched rafting! We indulged in more "if onlys" then. "If only the gear had arrived one day later," or, "If only the gear had not been stolen and they had left two days earlier, the river would not have been so high, and they might never have been upended." It seemed as if everything had conspired against Sarah.

Before reaching the place where we could see the accident site, we had walked through the cactus forest where Max Milligan had taken a picture of the group striking funny poses among the cacti. This was also the spot where the last known photograph of Sarah was taken – the one where she looked so happy. Pepé took a photograph of Mick and me in the same spot. I wept there and wept when we saw the river from above. We reached the river bank at 1.30 and, from then on, we kept stopping and starting for Mick to film everything and for Pepé to give us the narrative on film. "This is where the boat got stuck." "This is where they were all swimming." "This is where Sarah was floating down with no control going over the other rapid." "This is where I last saw her." "This is where we think she is," and so on.

I was appalled that anyone could go into this terrible, churning water with so many rocks to be injured by. Yet Pepé said that the water was less fierce this year. It was now considered a grade four whereas last year it was a grade five. How could the organisers have let people go in and how could the people agree? If I had been Sarah I would have flatly refused to enter the water.

Throughout the day we had seen only one man with three donkeys, two men with a mule and some donkeys and two lone men hiking. The place was truly remote and isolated. We had found the trekking physically demanding and emotionally painful even though part of us appreciated the beauty and wildness of this part of the Peruvian Andes. We reached the camp site that was in a beautiful valley just below the scene of the accident just before 3 pm, feeling tired. We enjoyed a salad, coca cola and pineapple juice and watched four Torrent ducks playing and swimming in the raging waters of the river. Pepé said it was unusual to see two pairs of these birds together and not common to see even one pair. We watched these fragile birds for a long time, enjoying their ability to swim against the turbulent waters. We felt they were a sign from Sarah, saying, "Be happy." Even though in my heart I did not believe in such signs, we watched out for them during the trip. Pepé believed in such signs and Mick said the birds were a sign for him that Sarah was in this place. At the very least, these playful, entertaining birds seemed like a symbol of hope. We decided to have the ceremony just above this spot the next day. Before dinner we walked among the Inca and pre-Inca ruins nearby. There were impressive acres of walled terraces. We could feel the spirit of these old civilisations and felt it was a good place for Sarah to be. If she had to die then she would have appreciated resting forever in this remote, wild, beautiful valley with the spirits of the Incas all around. That night we saw the Southern Cross above the river. This is Mick's favourite constellation. Again it seemed to be another sign that Sarah was there, especially when we saw a shooting star flash in front of the four points of the cross. It was a brilliant night lit by stars we felt we could touch. They would shine down on Sarah, night after night forever.

In the morning Mick picked a safe place in the river to bathe. The water was icy cold and took his breath away. He thought of Sarah's body being trapped, maybe a couple of hundred metres higher up the valley, and wondered whether any atom of her was in the water in which he bathed.

After a breakfast of bacon and eggs, Mick and I set off with Pepé the next morning at 9.20. We took the CD memorial tape, the Walkman and speakers together with some "presents" to throw into the river for Sarah. The place we decided to hold the ceremony was the spot where Sarah was presumed to be dead or at least unconscious before being pulled down into the depths. Pepé moved away, Mick set up the speakers on some rocks and we began.

First I told her about the memorial service in October and threw in a copy of the programme. Before we played the first song, "Don't Think Twice It's All Right", I said that Matthew had chosen the songs for the memorial service. We were overcome and held each other, both of us were crying. I then told Sarah about a book I had just read called *It's Not About the Bike* by Lance Armstrong, the American cyclist who overcame cancer and won the Tour de France on three occasions. I knew Sarah would have liked the book so I threw my copy into the river for her. We played song number two, beginning "I always flirt with death". A copy of

Anna's speech was thrown in next. I told Sarah that this was the best speech of the service. I read the last paragraph aloud before throwing it in the river. The third song, "Just Like Fred Astaire", came next. Simon, Jo, Cameron and Molly had given us a card and a photograph to go into the river so these went in along with a short piece I had written for The Compassionate Friends Newsletter. "I Wish I Were a Fisherman" was played and then Mick made a little speech for Sarah. He threw in a pen from his publishing company where Sarah had worked for 14 years and a postcard of Heron Island where Sarah had always wanted to go. Finally, we played the song I now always associate with Sarah, "Forever Young". During the ceremony there was one lonely swallow flying above and one beautiful yellow butterfly skimming the water. Once again, these appeared to be signs that Sarah was there and at peace. We finished at 10.05. Pepé came up and hugged us, saying how sorry he was. We felt it had been a good service but emotionally exhausting.

By this time the others had loaded up the animals and we left at 10.20. The first part of the route was fairly easy, but then we had to wade across a fast-flowing stream. Pepé took our backpacks across first, then he led me and then Mick. It was not easy finding our footing and keeping upright. This was only a stream yet we were made aware of the power of the water. Before lunch, Pepé took us into the house of a farmer he knew. The farm was by the riverbank. There had been a landslide there 20 days earlier and the farmer had lost land and fruit trees. He gave us wine and made us welcome. I realised he was talking (in Spanish) to Pepé about Sarah. Of course everyone along the river knew about her and about the reward for her body. As we left he said in Spanish, "You are welcome here at any time." I cried at this kindness.

After our picnic lunch and siesta, we set off at 2.20 and had a hard walk uphill for an hour, then up and downhill until 5.30 when we arrived back at the Chaupa camp. It had been the hardest day but we enjoyed the walking and felt fit. We had seen a few more people that day, a lone man in the morning, the farmer and his son, a man then a woman and her little girl with two sheep in the afternoon. We had also seen four schoolchildren in uniform way over on the other side of the river walking very quickly up a steep trail. Their school, said Pepé, was way above us on our side of the river so these children have to go down one mountain, cross the bridge and climb another mountain to get to and from school. We were impressed by this commitment to education. For dinner Raoul provided us with curry soup, spaghetti and tomato and mushroom sauce and crème caramel. He had managed chocolate pudding the night before! We wondered how he managed to produce such acceptable food on this difficult trip. He had one little stove to cook on. The father and son in charge of the

Figure 8.2 Barbara and Pepé wading through a stream that roared on to the mightier Cotahuasi

animals always did the washing up in the river. I watched them sometimes and everything was thoroughly cleaned. Feeling desperately tired I crawled into my sleeping bag at 8.10 and slept until 6 am.

Pancakes with maple syrup were provided for breakfast. Mick wanted to film and take photographs. The men were packing up and loading the animals so we did not leave until 9.15. We walked until noon with a few brief stops. We had crossed the most frightening path – a ridge a few inches wide across a steep, shale slope. This was the path I had travelled on horseback on the way out. This time we walked across with Pepé, one at a time. I thought, "Don't think about the drop, just go slowly, just put one foot in front of the other." It is a good thing I am not of a nervous disposition as this particular path would have made me very nervous.

Once past the difficult path, we met Edwin who had come out to greet us. At one point I rode on one of the mules (Mick refused to ride). I rode partly to be polite and partly because I was tired. Most of the trekking had been done between two and three thousand metres (six to ten thousand feet). Although we had not been affected by the altitude, we thought it must have made it harder for us as we live at sea level. We stopped for lunch at 1.30 and watched three crazy workmen on the other side of the river knocking off boulders from the hillside to make a platform to fix a water channel. It looked a high-risk operation. At 2 pm we set off for the final walk to the mule and donkey parking place. Even Mick rode for some of this last 40-minute trek. The place where we left the animals was busy and lively. Some workmen were building a new bridge. Just the wire construction was in place with no tarmac covering. Mick, Pepé, Edwin and I walked over one at a time. Mick and I were the first "gringos" to cross this bridge.

We watched the locals with donkeys, mules and horses. Our animals were unloaded. I felt relieved for them, they had worked so hard, particularly the three donkeys. Our van had to be loaded and we left for the 35-minute journey back to Cotahuasi town and the Hostal Chavez, arriving at 3.30 pm. We had used our last soles (Peruvian money) to tip Marcos and Luis (the men looking after the animals) so, after putting the bags in our room, we went to change dollars and phone Anna. She was pleased to hear from us. I think people at home had been anxious about the trip. They were not sure we would cope.

Just before 5 pm, Pepé, Edwin, Raoul, Mick and I set off with the owner of the hostel, his wife and daughter to drive to the thermal baths. Sarah had been there in May 2000 and we had all been there the year before when Rosie had been the centre of attention. If white tourists were unusual, white children were particularly unusual. We swam in the hot water. It was hard to swim for long in the high temperature; we shampooed our hair and were back at the hotel at 7.20. We went out to dinner in town that evening and all agreed that Raoul's cooking was better.

On Friday June 1st we set off at 5.45 for the long journey back to Arequipa. We breakfasted at 7.00 in a spectacular spot high in the mountains. Later we saw chinchilla, vicuna and a vulture. More driving until 2.30 when we deviated from our route to go to a museum of petroglyphs (rock carvings) from pre-Inca times. I would have preferred to go straight to Arequipa. Raoul prepared our final lunch at the entrance to the museum. We saw the carvings. As the area was grey and desolate, I felt a wave of depression wash over me. I did not want to be there. I was thinking of Sarah and this place was not associated with her. We left at 4.25 for a very tedious journey to Arequipa. In the morning, over a 6-hour period, we saw only two vehicles, one was high up on a mountain a long way away and one was stuck in a stream. After leaving the museum, we were behind one truck after another all the way. We reached the hotel at 7.30 pm. We showered and changed.

An hour later, we met up again. Mick and I took Pepé, Edwin and Raoul to dinner at Leonides (where we had had a good lunch a few days earlier). We enjoyed the meal. A friend of Pepé's came in, a kayaker and guide. We discussed Sarah and her trip. Pepé said Sarah was not just a client but a journalist who was writing an article about the trip. He implied that she was allowed to go, despite her relative inexperience, because she was a journalist. I was sceptical, thinking Amazonas Explorer (and other companies of course) would take anyone who could pay. We knew that young Chris, the last to be rescued from the raft Sarah was on, had no rafting experience at all. We tipped Edwin and Raoul, leaving Pepé until the next day when we would see him again.

We had a lazy day on Saturday June 2nd. Most of the morning was taken up trying to change money, having my black sandals cleaned by a local lad who did an excellent job, buying stamps and writing cards. Pepé joined us at midday. He was going to Lima that afternoon and said he hoped to meet us there the next day for dinner. We tipped Pepé then lazed around for the afternoon. I was rather bored as I do not like being lazy but I suppose we needed one such day. It was election day in Peru so there was a problem getting alcohol as its sale is forbidden on that day. We had water with dinner and one beer back at the hotel. The previous trip had also been at election time. In 2000, Fujimori had won. He had run off to Japan in disgrace during the year and now Toledo won the election. The local people we met seemed happy with the result.

I wanted to be home. We set off for Lima on the 3rd and for home on the 4th, but we were delayed in Miami. The flight from Lima to Miami was fine. We then took a British Airways flight from Miami to London. Forty minutes into the flight, however, we were told we had to return to Miami. One engine had overheated. We flew around jettisoning fuel. Some people were frightened. I was not as I believed it was possible to fly with only one engine functioning. We spent the night at a good hotel in Miami, care of British Airways, shopped the next morning and tried to make the most of our enforced, unexpected stay. Next day we flew home safely and were met by Matthew at Heathrow.

So we had survived the first year and the trek. Some people said to us "Did it bring you peace?" or "Did it help you achieve closure?" (a meaningless and hateful term to me). I was irritated by these statements, we did not achieve peace or closure. At the time we achieved emotional turmoil and physical exhaustion. The trip was something we felt we had to do. In retrospect, it was helpful to see what Sarah would have seen during her last days. We were pleased that, given she had to die, she was in such a beautiful place. We liked the valley and the ruins around. We felt her presence there although that may well have been wishful thinking. We continue to miss her, yearn for her, think about her and talk about her. We are still angry with her for going on the trip and causing us this anguish. We are sad that her nieces are left without their wonderful auntie. Rosie will always remember her but Francesca will have nothing but the most fragmentary memories. We still have not been successful in getting a death certificate. We continue to be less bothered by the unimportant things in life, like missing a train or losing a bag, and we still feel an immediate bond with any other parents who tell us they have lost a child.

Figure 8.3 Mick and Barbara with their recently published book about the loss of Sarah. (Image credit: Bury Free Press)

We thought out hearts were broken when we lost our firstborn child. Our hearts have healed, or at least the open wound has become a scar. We cry very readily. The disaster in the United States on September 11th affected almost all the world, but we felt particularly affected as we knew how parents losing adult children would feel; particularly those who did not have a body to bury. Yet we felt their situation was worse than ours, for men had caused the deaths of the people in New York, Washington and Pennsylvania. Sarah chose her white water rafting trip and was not the victim of brutality or terror. At times her death seems inevitable, at times we cannot really believe she is dead. We can laugh, enjoy ourselves, work, play, sleep, eat, despite this wound. The first year is hard, but as all bereaved parents say, "You learn to live with it." This is a cliché but it is also true. Sarah, we miss you, we love you, we will never forget you. You were our joy, our treasure, our precious gift and we will try to live our lives better because of you.

Mick wrote several poems to Sarah throughout the book. His final poem appeared at the end, and this is what he said, imagining Sarah was talking to him:

Epilogue

I've been talking to you, Sarah,

For four years now

Since you died,

And I'm sorry to say this

But I feel as though I've been talking to myself.

You certainly don't answer me

And I have to fill in all the gaps

Where your words ought to be.

So, I'm going to ask you now,

Here is your chance:

I want you to take over

And speak to me.

I'll say this dad

I didn't want to die on that day

And in fact I didn't think I would.

OK, I was scared

As we all were

But I thought I would be alright.

We had practised all the safety procedures

And although the river looked terrifying

I felt secure with my mates.

And then there were all the others

Waiting down river to rescue anyone who might fall in.

It happened straight away.

I just made a joke to the others standing on the bank,

We pushed off

And immediately the boat was sucked round, and

Try as we might we could not right it;

And soon it reared up and we were in the rapid.

Christ almighty Dad!

Turmoil, pressure, biting cold,

Pain.

You name it

It was all there.

Panic!

I couldn't breathe and I couldn't help myself!

Was it my head, my neck, my back?

Why couldn't I move?

I was moving alright!

At a huge pace

As the rapid sucked me on and down

And up and down again.

Breathing was so bloody difficult,

Choking as the rescuers flashed by!

I was swept along past peaceful inlets,

Between vast rocks.

Viewed from above

I was a stick someone's thrown into fast running water,

Except that it wasn't at all jolly

Bobbing up and down, believe me!

Yes, the would-be rescuers were right,

I did at one point put up a bit of a fight

And got into the right position

But that was not enough

Because I couldn't control my body

To get to a bank.

Just speeding down and up and sometimes round
And sometimes into a rock
Or scraping on gravel.

Well, you know me dad.

I can take so much
And then I have to say "Sod it!"
I can't go on.

And so I stopped struggling and drifted
With the rapid
And looked up at the lovely blue sky.

And the lovely high mountains
And the hot sun
And I let myself become part of it.

Don't worry about it Dad
It was peaceful in the end.

The pain had gone
And the fear.

It was a relief really,
No more silly anger
Or ambition
Or fear
Or regrets.

Just me and the sky and the mountains and sun,
And rocks and, as I rolled over for the last time,
The river.

Part Two

In Part Two of this book I write principally about life after retirement but I also take the opportunity to fill gaps in the text of earlier chapters that are inevitable when one is writing one's memoirs. Some memories come flooding back after one has written a chapter and I don't want to leave these out if they contribute to a broader understanding of my life. So the reader will find more about certain happenings in my earlier life and more about family and friends and my travels that were not initially included in Part One where they would have sat well enough had I remembered them at the time of first writing.

9 Return to work and my final years as a professional

I mentioned a little about returning to work in the previous chapter but will say more here. It was very hard for me to return after Sarah's death, I felt I had too many troubles of my own to deal with other people's problems. I almost retired, and kept saying I would retire, but I never did. I went back to work after three weeks and saw Julie, my secretary, who gasped when she saw me and said I had shrunken. I knew I had lost weight and I felt even smaller than my tiny five feet in height. At first I could not do much apart from sit in my room and cry. The first time of doing anything was so difficult. This included the first trip to the post room, the first time to the canteen, the first talk I went to – everything was such an effort. I persevered and gradually things became easier although, as I said in the last chapter, it was six months before I managed a whole day with no tears and a year before I could stay at work for the whole day. I wanted to be in touch with other bereaved parents and I wondered how I would get through life without Sarah. One funny thing happened at the Oliver Zangwill Centre when I first went back. Jon Evans, who was still there then as our clinical manager, had told the patients to be good to me in my troubled state. I was in the kitchen making a cup of coffee when one of the clients, a man with severe memory problems, came up to me having just read in his notebook that he had to be kind, and said, "We are all with you. Barbara." I replied, "Except Sarah," to which he said, "Why, what happened to her?" It was sad and funny at the same time and so typical of a person with the amnesic syndrome.

In April 2001, almost a year after Sarah died, I saw the London Marathon on television and vowed that one day I would run that for Sarah. I tried several times to get a place through the national ballot but wasn't successful. Some charities have their own slots and you can get a place for one of them provided you collect a certain amount of money. I wanted to run for Sarah though and collect money for The Compassionate Friends (TCF), who did not have their own slot. In 2007, I applied again for the 2008 marathon, a centenary year (the marathon began in 1908). I was unlucky again in the national ballot but, because it was 100 years since the first marathon, an extra 1,000 places were being given away and I was offered one of those. When the letter arrived, I was scared. I had never run on the road before and I would be 66 years old when the marathon took place in April. We had some time before accepting the offer and I was just off to the United States to give another workshop so I told myself I would decide while I was away. I realised I might never get another chance so accepted the offer and replied before the closing date saying I would take up the place.

I bought myself a book about how to run a marathon. It had programmes for beginners and novices as well as for more experienced people. The programmes were 18 weeks long and I just had time to fit them all in before the actual race in April. Of course I followed the beginner's programme, which started off with a three-mile run followed by two miles (yes, going backwards); the number of miles to be run in the training gradually increased and typically went backwards and forwards. We were told to have one day off a week and one day doing something other than running. I swam on those days. I followed the programme as carefully as possible. I was travelling a great deal by now and actually

Figure 9.1 Barbara running in the London Marathon. Ecstatic as ever when challenged

trained in eight different countries: the UK, of course, France, the Gambia, Senegal, Hawaii in the United States, Fiji, Australia and New Zealand. I think this was a record for the number of countries trained in. In Fiji I was on a cruise with Betty Glisky, a colleague from the United States, and wondered how to fit in my run. I decided to run around the top deck early in the morning and, as I did so, a steward came rushing up to tell me to stop as the first-class passengers were sleeping below! That meant I could not run on the ship. We went ashore each day so I had to do my "run" on land but the sand was too soft to run on, so I made do with fast walking instead.

The longest run in the programme was 20 miles even though the marathon itself is 26.2 miles. The book said not to run more than 20 miles during training and wait until the actual day before running the whole 26.2 miles, or else it would be too exhausting. I was in New Zealand when it was time for the 20-mile run and staying with a friend, Jenni Ogden, who lived on the very beautiful Great Barrier Island. I explained to Jenni that I was training for the marathon and needed to run 20 miles while I was staying with her. She said not to worry and she would take me to a beach for my run. I knew I could not run on sand but the beach Jenni took me to was very different from the soft sand in Fiji. This was hard-packed sand and so beautiful, the most beautiful place I had trained in. Jenni and her husband John took me and waited for me – I am slow and always did a mixture of running and walking so they had to wait for quite a while in order for me to complete the 20 miles. In the whole time, though, no other person appeared on that beach. New Zealand is, indeed, a wonderful country.

I arrived back home and it was nearly time for race day. I had to go to collect my bits and pieces from ExCel in London a few days before the race. As I walked in I heard the marathon tune that is always on the television on marathon day. This made me feel very emotional. My main worry was that I would not be able to attach my electronic shoelaces correctly. These are needed to record the runners going over the check points to confirm they have really completed the course. I went home with my laces and details of where to meet. I decided to dedicate each mile to a bereaved family and their lost son or daughter. The first and last miles were for Sarah and the others for people we had met on our journey of grief. I wrote the names down so I would know who I running for at the start of the next mile. Mick, Anna, Carol and Francesca came with me to London, we stayed in a hotel overnight and I went by underground to the right spot. Underground trips were free that day to all marathon runners. Other members of the family planned to be at various points along the route but it was so difficult I only saw them at one spot, just before the 12-

mile marker. There is a marker at each mile so everyone knows how far they have run and how many miles still to complete. I was told to drink plenty of water before the start but I think I drank too much as I had to stop several times to pee. The weather wasn't very good that day. I knew that we would discard clothes along the way and leave these for bystanders to collect and wear. There was, of course, someone to help with the shoelaces so I needn't have worried about them. Mick's last words were that the Ethiopians and Kenyans had heard I was going to run and that they were very anxious! Ha, ha. Francesca, aged 11 at that point, really thought her grandmother was going to win!

It took ages to get going but eventually we were underway. I loved the crowd and the atmosphere. There were people and families along the whole route, white families, black families, Asian families. A wonderful multi-cultural experience. Everyone wanted us to do well. It was a magnificent gathering of the best of humanity. As well as the water stations at every mile and signs telling us how many miles to go, several people had things to give us, biscuits and chocolates and slices of banana. I took a piece of banana every time I saw one as my body craved bananas during my run. I realised afterwards that it was because they contained potassium and that is what I needed at the time. One woman living right on the route allowed people into her house to use her toilet! This was a great gift only appreciated, I think, by the marathon runners themselves, especially the women. I didn't need a toilet at that point but had to stop three times during the race – and queue – because of all the water I was drinking. I was envious of the men who peed at the side of the road whereas the women had to queue for the facilities! That slowed me up so I took a little over the six hours I was planning on. My finish time was six hours and seven minutes. I realise this is very slow in comparison with many people but my goal was to finish and I achieved that goal. About halfway through I saw my family and held up my arms in greeting. Mick took a photograph of this and, because, I am looking so victorious, it looks as if I had won the race. I wasn't looking so good at the end though, by which time I was walking more than running.

Most people wore a t-shirt with their name and charity on. I had a shirt with my name, a photo of Sarah and the TCF logo. People called out all along the route, "Come on Barbara, give us a smile," or "Come on, Barbara, you are half way," or "Only five miles to go" and "Only two miles to go" and "Only half a mile to go," by which time I thought it is too far, I can't do it. I knew I would do it though partly because I didn't want to let down any of the families I had dedicated to their children, and partly because I didn't know how to give the money back. At the end of each mile I was boosted a little, thinking I have finished that mile for Eleanor or Joe or Madeleine or whoever, and now I can start for (whoever was next on the list). I had collected £8,000 for TCF from people all over the world.

The end came and my legs turned to jelly but I had finished! The last part of the race requires the participants to go up a very gentle incline (which felt like a mountain) so somebody could cut the electronic laces off. My legs had turned to jelly as soon as I stopped so climbing this tiny incline was very difficult. We were given a bag of goodies and a finisher's shirt, which I still have, and we then had to find our families. I phoned Carol's mobile. She had inadvertently put it on silent, but in the end we met up. I was so shattered, I could not even put on my tracksuit bottoms, which Anna had in her bag. She had to dress me, much to the astonishment of 11-year-old Francesca who had never seen her grandmother being dressed before. We arrived home somehow and for the next few days I was stiff and sore but with no harm done and no joint problems – due perhaps to the mixture of running and walking. I loved the marathon. In particular, I loved the people and the atmosphere – all those thousands of onlookers sending out goodwill to every runner is good for one's soul.

The marathon I took part in came eight years after Sarah's death so I was well back to work by then. I had taken almost a year of doing relatively little apart from examining the occasional PhD, writing the odd chapter and paper and seeing the occasional patient. I had great sympathy for the families of people with brain injuries and there were similarities between their losses and mine. We were both bereaved in a way. Although they had the person there, in many ways they had lost the person they once knew. We both grieved for the person that was no longer in our lives. I used to think that if Sarah had survived with a traumatic brain injury or anoxic brain damage due to shortage of oxygen caused by near drowning, then I would know what to do, where to go for help and what questions to ask. I am not so sure of this now though. I have seen parents watch their loved ones remain unchanged for many years, especially parents at the Raphael Hospital. I talk more of this in the following chapter. Even soon after Sarah's death, however, my view was challenged. I knew a very good American speech and language pathologist, Audrey Holland. Her son, Ben, had been murdered in Tucson about two years before Sarah died. I remember hearing about it at the time and thinking, "How awful!" but I did not really appreciate how Audrey must have felt. She contacted me when she heard about Sarah and, of course, as she was a bereaved parent, her words meant a great deal to me. When I said that had Sarah survived with brain damage it would have been easier for me, Audrey disagreed as her son had sustained such terrible brain injuries, she thought it best that he didn't survive. I can, of course, appreciate her views and think now that we are in a better place than many relatives who undergo very prolonged grief when their loved ones survive with a disorder of consciousness. The bottom line, however, is that we don't get to choose what happens to those we love. Whatever life chucks at us, we have to deal with.

My first holiday trip after Sarah died was to Sarawak in Borneo in August 2000. I was going to a conference in Hong Kong with Agnes Shiel and decided to go on a trip first. I thought I would manage Hong Kong as there would be colleagues there who would understand. Agnes would be there for a start. In addition, I had been to Hong Kong several times, I had ex-students working there and other people I felt comfortable with. I wanted another holiday before the work in Hong Kong and decided to go with "Explore", a travel company I had been with three times before, including a wonderful holiday to Jordan with Sarah at the end of 1997/ beginning of 1998. The only trip that was in South East Asia and fitted in with the Hong Kong dates was a ten-day trip to Sarawak. It would be the first trip alone I had taken since Sarah died. Although an experienced traveller with few nerves, I was not sure how I would cope with Sarawak, which was an unknown. Before I left, Agnes said, "Are you looking forward to Sarawak?" I said that I had mixed feelings about it and then I started to cry again. I never knew when the tears would overcome me. I flew to Hong Kong, stayed in The Crowne Plaza and left some things there as I was returning to Hong Kong for the conference after Malaysia. I telephoned Mick and cried on the phone remembering that Sarah had been with me in Hong Kong about two years earlier. She enjoyed it immensely. She said she loved Hong Kong and we should bring Rosie as Rosie liked shopping so much. I decided to try to enjoy the trip to Malaysia for Sarah's sake. My travelling now would be for her. I would try to see new places through Sarah's eyes. I left for Kuching in Malaysia on August 15th. Kuching means Cat in Malay and that pleased me. I met up with my group and managed reasonably well. At one point though, one of the women asked me how many children I had. Of course that set me off crying. I said three but one died. I went to run off but she stopped me, she held my arm and said, "Tell me about her." That was exactly the right thing to say and we bonded after that. I asked if she knew bereaved people as she handled everything so well. She said no but she was a mother. I managed the trip mostly trekking through jungle, which I liked. I flew back to Hong Kong, met up with Agnes and enjoyed the conference. Travelling without Sarah though was hard in those first few years, even though we visited some great places and particularly loved a few safaris we could afford.

We've been on some great safaris and they are probably our favourite holidays. You never know what you are going to see as your truck twists and turns along the trails. Who is going to be first to spot something? Who is going to get the best camera shot? Will it be on my side of the van or the other? Will the creature be dangerous or nervous? Will it be moving or still, eating, sleeping or hunting? Staring, stalking? Alone or in a group? The first really impressive animal we saw was a Martial Eagle in Botswana. We came across it in a shady, wooded place. It was right by the side of our truck and you could have touched it, it was so close. It wasn't at all afraid of us, perhaps just a little suspicious while it was standing on top of a huge monitor lizard, which we measured in comparison to ourselves. It was five feet, as long as me – and much bigger than the eagle! The lizard could not move, as the eagle held it with its amazing talons, slowly pulling out thin entrails from the lizard's stomach with its beak and eating them, a very slow death! We stayed there for longer than half an hour and the lizard made no response at all as its entrails were pulled out to astonishing lengths. Although the eagle was not particularly bothered by us, apart from giving us a stony, golden stare every so often, it was definitely disturbed by a group of smaller eagles that were flying around obviously sensing that something edible was down below. The eagle kept looking up at them suspiciously and then spreading its vast wings to completely hide the five foot lizard from their view. How impressive was that! Those huge wings!

Martial Eagles are native to sub-Saharan Africa and are one of the largest and most powerful of the eagles. They eat mammals, reptiles and birds. They are one of the most endangered bird species in the world: because they attack livestock and game, local farmers and game wardens kill them and they are currently classified as "vulnerable to extinction". Their total length can vary from 31 to 38 inches and their wingspan from 6 feet 2 inches to 8 feet 6 inches. I shall never forget our eagle, its huge eyes, almost as big as a human's, and their piercing gaze at us.

The next impressive animal we saw was a lion, which was part of a drama we had just missed, but were able to put together with the aid of our guide. This lion was magnificent and in top condition as he stretched to his full height on his back legs, spraying frequently and looking into the distance where we could just see two lions disappearing slowly while turning frequently to look back towards what was obviously a place that was once theirs. He was huge and obviously in top condition with almost a blue tone to his body and a magnificent golden mane. One thing though was that he had a huge open wound running across his nose, obviously a wound from the fight that must have taken place between him and the other two. Then we noticed a few cubs that came out of the bush close to the lion and he chased them back in. My naïve interpretation of what had just happened was that there had been a fight and that another male had been victorious and was walking away with the mother of the cubs, leaving our male alone with the cubs. I couldn't have been more wrong as this could never happen in this way. The guide explained that our lion would have chased off the other two lions after some kind of fight; they may both have been females and their cubs had been left behind, and it was almost certain that the lion in front of us would in time kill the cubs as part of his capture of a new territory.

One more memorable incident I have selected is the occasion when we came across a pack of African dogs, an animal I particularly like, and had been hoping to see when it seemed hopeless as our four hours was nearly completed. Our truck was making its way along a broad track, obviously one of the main avenues on the way back to our camp site, when the driver got a call from another guide in another truck. He didn't say anything to us except to indicate excitement as he turned the truck around and we started to head away from home base at a speed which brought a certain amount of discomfort and clinging on! As we began to climb a steep slope we saw in the distance a pack of animals loping along the side of the track and towards us. Our driver stopped and turned the vehicle round so it was facing the direction the animals were heading towards. Soon they were beside us and we started getting some great pictures of these impressive dogs with their huge ears, dramatic colours, long legs, lolloping tongues and big grins. We travelled with them for some distance until they stopped by the side of a vast puddle in which they rolled, keeping watching all the time towards a distance to our left and off route. It seemed to us that the dogs had a group purpose, their excitement mounted and showed in their body movements and the noise they were making. Then, with what seemed like one group signal, they all increased their speed towards something we could not see. We followed in the truck, holding on to our head gear and bumping up and down in our seats. We had become part of the chase! This was extraordinary and vastly exhilarating as the truck seemed to fly along with the dogs leading the way, some of them veering to the right and others to the left. Then the territory began to thicken and became too uneven so the truck had to stop and we watched as the dogs continued towards their prey, which we never did see! The next day we did meet up with the dogs again, this time they were sleeping in a hollow, panting in the heat, and with full bellies.

On another trip to Singapore in 2003, I decided to write the book about losing Sarah. I had read things by other bereaved parents but almost all were religious. We are not. We sometimes call ourselves atheists and sometimes humanists. We do not believe there is a god or a supreme being and we do not believe in an afterlife. We do believe people have to be good to one another and "do unto others as we would want then to do unto us". We think that any disaster could happen to anyone. We cannot choose the colour of our skin, where we were born or what religion our parents have but we can choose to be good people and we try, not always successfully, to do this.

Anyway, back to the book for Sarah. I wanted to write something for the non-believers. Our grief is as deep and full of anguish as anyone's and we love our children as much as the next person so I wanted this in print. I started on the long journey to Singapore and wrote a chunk of the book on the plane. When I returned home, Mick decided to co-write it with me. We used my journal to capture the early terrible days and he wrote a more balanced view from three years later. Thus, each chapter starts with Mick's view for 2003 and continues with my part from 2000. The book was published in 2004 after a bit of a struggle trying to find a publisher who would do it. I had not written the book as therapy but, when finished, I realised it was actually very therapeutic.

I said earlier that Matthew and Andrea had two lovely boys, whom, of course, Sarah never knew. She would have loved them as she loved all children and would have been very good with them. Sammy, the elder of the two boys was born in October 2005, over five years since Sarah's death. We were actually in Venezuela with Matthew when we discovered Andrea was pregnant. We had been to a meeting in South America, met up with Matt and travelled together for a short holiday to Margarita Island. Matt phoned Andrea one evening and came to us in a state of shock saying Andrea thinks she is pregnant. He phoned later when Andrea confirmed the news so we all went to celebrate. In October that year, I was flying to Bogota in Colombia when I got the news that Sammy had been born. I told the stewardess on the plane and she brought me some champagne. I travelled from Bogota to Santiago de Chile after the meeting in Bogota to meet my new grandson. Max, his younger brother, was born in May 2007. Like most grandmothers I am very proud of my four grandchildren and my great granddaughter and will say more about each of them in Chapter 11.

So I did manage to lead a meaningful life after going through our awful tragedy. I published books, worked on more tests, travelled widely, had a rehabilitation centre named after me in Quito, Ecuador and a prize set up in my name. More of these things in Chapter 11. For the moment I am just reflecting on that scruffy little girl running around the streets of Brixton just after the Second World War, having no idea what was in store for her in future years! Her learning disabled mum and war-wounded dad would not have been able to imagine the life their daughter was going to lead as an academic, clinician, wife, mother and world traveller.

10 Retirement and post retirement
The Raphael Hospital

When I was working for the Medical Research Council (MRC), there was a compulsory retirement age of 65. In fact people could choose to stay on until the September after their sixty-fifth birthday. I chose this option so I left shortly before my sixty-sixth birthday. I believe compulsory retirement is no longer legal, but I was pleased at the time that I did not have to make the decision on whether or not to leave. I had a lump sum paid to me and, after retirement, I was able to choose invitations that appealed to me and reject those that did not. I now reject invitations to examine a PhD as "I have retired" but I accept many invitations to lecture abroad as I still like travelling. In the few months before retirement, the MRC organised a two-day workshop on retirement to which spouses and partners were also invited. The workshop covered financial and practical matters together with other issues about retirement. Mick and I thought highly of this workshop, although in the long run it was less relevant to me than to others as I am still working 12 years later.

The first person to persuade me to work for a day each week in my retirement was my colleague, Narinder Kapur. I went to Addenbrooke's Hospital in Cambridge to help Narinder. While there, I saw patients, supervised assistants and helped to write papers. One paper we published together was about an American woman who had attempted suicide by shooting herself through the mouth. She survived, although she sustained brain damage of course. The area of damage was in the frontal lobes; these areas are responsible for many things including planning, organisation, problem-solving, selective attention, personality, behaviour and emotions. In fact she did surprisingly well in many ways and the depression leading to the suicide attempt cleared. She had no memory problems and, on tests of executive functioning, she was able to manage some tasks involving planning and problem-solving. She had great difficulty, however, on one problem-solving test. We published this paper in 2009

(Kapur et al., 2009). We could not follow her up as she returned to the United States after a few months.

It was not long before I was asked to return to the Oliver Zangwill Centre (OZC) for one day a week and, apart from when I was travelling abroad somewhere, I kept this up until April 2018 when I cut down to two days a month. It has recently increased to three days a month. I continued (and still continue) to publish either alone or with OZC colleagues. One of the books I like is one I published with Jill Winegardner and Fiona Ashworth in 2014, although, of course, we were planning and working on that for two or three years before publication. The book is called *Life After Brain Injury: Survivors' Stories* (Wilson, Winegardner and Ashworth, 2014). In this book 17 survivors of different kinds of brain injury, and with different outcomes, write their stories. Each chapter is written partly by the survivor and partly by a neuropsychologist and summarises what they think of rehabilitation. Two of the ex-clients reported did extremely well and returned to high-powered positions, some of them still needed full-time care, and one man's treatment was considered to be a failure. We included his story because it is important to learn about failures as well as successes.

I think the 2014 book is a testament to the value of listening to what patients have to say about their treatment and progress, and Lucy Kennedy, from the publishing house, was persuaded to think similarly, asking me to become series editor for a whole range of Survivors' Stories books. I co-authored three more in the series and others have contributed too. We have a book from a survivor of severe prosopagnosia (face blindness) by Wilson, Robertson and Mole (2015); one about a man who was assaulted by a gang and remained with a disorder of consciousness for 19 months before waking up and doing well (Wilson, Dhamapurkar and Rose, 2016); one about life after encephalitis (Easton, 2016); one about a man with locked-in syndrome (Wilson, Allen, Rose and Kubikova, 2018). At least four other Survivors Stories are in the pipeline, including one with another ex OZC client, Alex, who survived a rare brain tumour (Jelly, Helmy and Wilson, 2019).

Perhaps two other books are worth mentioning here. One is *Neuropsychological Rehabilitation: The International Handbook* (Wilson, Winegardner, van Heugten and Ownsworth, 2017). This book began a few years ago when Lucy Kennedy asked me if I knew anyone who might be interested in publishing a handbook of Neuropsychological Rehabilitation. I said that I would do it with help from others. I chose Jill Winegardner, an American citizen working in the UK, Caroline van Heugten from The Netherlands and Tamara Ownsworth from Australia to be co-editors with me. We emailed each other and agreed a structure and who would be responsible for overseeing each chapter. It was also agreed that each chapter would be read by two people and that Jill would read everything. So, we had four women editors from around the world. Everyone pulled their weight and the edited book was submitted on time! This was a huge achievement given we had 45 chapters with over 100 contributors from 18 different countries. It is a truly international book, unlike some which describe themselves as international but turn out to be a collection of chapters written mainly by a group of authors known to each other, many of whom work in the same country.

One of the most successful books in terms of sales was published by Guilford Press in New York and is called *The Brain Injury Rehabilitation Workbook* (Winson, Wilson and Bateman, 2017). Rochelle Serwator persuaded me to embark on this book during one of our meetings of the International Neuropsychological Society in the United States. I thought one of the occupational therapists (OTs) working at the OZC at the time, Rachel Winson, would be the best person to lead this project. Not only was Rachel very good, she had also previously worked in publishing before training as an OT, and was one of the people who read the manuscript of our international handbook, making some very sensible comments on that. Rachel accepted the project and co-edited the book with the help of Andrew Bateman (then clinical manager of the OZC) and myself. The chapters were written by members of the OZC staff. *The Brain Injury Rehabilitation Workbook* provides advice and exercises for those rehabilitation workers who are not part of a team and may be working alone. Each chapter in the book is structured in the same or almost the same way, namely: 1. A brief introduction; 2.The theoretical background and models; 3. Neuroanatomy; 4. Common presenting problems; 5. Assessment; 6. Making the links (with other problems); 7. Rehabilitation: the evidence; 8. Understanding and exploring the problem with clients; 9. Developing strategies; 10. Bringing it all together; 11. A case study; and 12. Photocopiable worksheets.

By this time I was also working at the Raphael Hospital, called until recently "The Raphael Medical Centre" (RMC). Employment here started in 2008. The director was Dr Gerhard Florschutz and his deputy at that time was Tanesh Bhugobaun. I had met Tanesh occasionally at meetings. Soon after retirement, he contacted me to ask if I would be interested in doing occasional work at the RMC. At first I said "no" as I had just retired and it was situated in Kent over 100 miles away from my home. He persisted and said would I at least visit. I agreed to do this and drove down one day to see the centre. It is the only anthroposophic hospital in the UK. The philosophy of anthroposophic medicine is based on Rudolph Steiner principles. It follows an approach which believes in the integration of mind, body and spirit to support people suffering from complex neurological disabilities including physical, cognitive and behavioural impairments. It partly complements and partly replaces mainstream medicine. Practitioners employ a variety of treatment techniques including massage, exercise, counselling, and the use of anthroposophic drugs, which are similar to homeopathic drugs. Thus, some of the therapies are unlike those found in more traditional hospitals and rehabilitation services. Of course, I am not a follower of anthroposophic medicine and would not be expected to participate in any of its treatments at the RMC. I would be allowed to continue my scientific, evidence-based work there, in an institution where compassion was shown to patients and where the staff were not allowed to give up on anybody.

I found the place with little trouble but while parking I backed into a giant terracotta flower pot and cracked it! I felt terrible and apologised profusely but was told not to worry and I noticed that, by the time I left at the end of the day, the flower pot had been replaced. Apart from the broken flower pot, the visit was successful and I was asked if I would work one day a week there. Again I said "no", feeling it was too far away from home, but I did offer to do some one-day workshops. I did two or three of these over the next few weeks and, during one of these days, I was asked to see one of the patients to give some advice. That was it; I became hooked and soon starting going down one day a week to see patients.

Before me there had been a clinical neuropsychologist who went in to the RMC sometimes but many of his reports said "patient untestable"! Remember that I was told never to say a patient was untestable so I was rather shocked at this. There are tests for patients with a disorder of consciousness, tests for people who are severely cognitively impaired and tests for people who have severe language problems. Even if it is difficult or impossible to administer a published test, one can do an observational assessment. Later, a full-time clinical neuropsychologist was appointed, Dr Anita Rose, who was very active in the Multiple Sclerosis Society and had also worked in brain injury. When I was at the hospital we worked together for a few years and published together.

I found the patients at the RMC fascinating, I was never bored and each day flew past very quickly. Until May 2019, I went down to The Raphael three or four times a month. It is now called the Raphael Hospital. I began to see patients with prolonged disorders of consciousness (DOC) and this became one of my main interests. People with a disorder of consciousness are either in coma, or in the vegetative state (VS) or in the minimally conscious state (MCS). Those in coma show no verbal response, do not obey commands and do not open their eyes spontaneously or to stimulation (Teasdale and Jennett, 1974). Those in the VS open their eyes but show no response to the environment and show no apparent awareness of themselves. Families do not like the term "vegetative" and frequently misinterpret it as "vegetable" (see Wilson, Dhamapurkar and Rose, 2016). The European task force on DOC (Laureys et al., 2010) has recommended the term "unresponsive wakefulness syndrome" (UWS) to replace that of "vegetative state". To date this has only happened in a few cases. Steven Laureys' group in Belgium, for example, do use the UWS instead of VS. People in the MCS also open their eyes and show inconsistent, but reproducible, responses above the level of spontaneous or reflexive behaviour, which indicate some degree of interaction with their surroundings (Royal College of Physicians, 2013). Thus, there is behavioural evidence of self- or environmental awareness. Although I had seen a few people with a DOC and had supervised Agnes's PhD on this topic, it was not until I was at the RMC that I began to see these people regularly and interacted with their families too.

As the vast majority of people regain full consciousness or open their eyes within four weeks if they have not died, the ones I saw at the RMC were either vegetative or in the MCS. One of the patients I saw with a DOC was Gary, a young man beaten by a gang of youths while trying to protect his father. I mentioned him above as we wrote a book about him (Wilson, Dhamapurkar and Rose, 2016). Gary came to the Raphael four months after the attack while he was in a VS (or UWS) and he remained so for a number of months. He then progressed to the MCS where he remained for a further five months. Thus for19 months he had a DOC. The prognosis for such people is poor and I remember saying to Gary's mother that he would show some improvement but she probably would not get the old Gary back. She said she did not believe me, to which I replied that I hoped she was right and I would love to be proved wrong. She did indeed prove me wrong. One day, as I was walking down the corridor at the RMC, I saw Gary in his wheelchair. I said "Good morning," as I always do, and to my great surprise Gary said "Good morning" back. Remember I had known him for 15 months since his admission to the RMC and I had assessed him several times. He had never spoken before. I did a double take and said to his carer "What happened?" She said that Gary had woken up. From that moment he progressed rapidly. He had rehabilitation for three years and went home, walking and talking. His was a fairy tale story and we were so impressed with his progress that we decided to write the book about him (Wilson, Dhamapurkar and Rose, 2016).

I also saw people with very rare and unusual syndromes which I had not seen or even heard of in my years of clinical practice. One man had cerebral salt-wasting disease. When I first heard of this I thought it was a made-up syndrome so I went straight back to my room to check it out on Google. It does indeed exist, and is described in Wikipedia (2019) as:

> a rare endocrine condition featuring a low blood sodium concentration and dehydration in response to injury (trauma) or the presence of tumors in or surrounding the brain. In this condition, the kidney is functioning normally but excreting excessive sodium (Yee, Burns and Wijdicks, 2010). The condition was initially described in 1950 (Peters et al., 1950). Its cause and management remain controversial.

That was certainly not the only rare condition I had never heard of and which required me to check. I was referred a patient with Alexander's Disease, a rare form of childhood dementia. It is a slowly progressing neurodegenerative disease mostly involving the midbrain and cerebellum. It typically affects infants and children, causing developmental delay (Wilson, Vargha-Khadem and Florschutz, 2018). This young woman was diagnosed at the age of 5 years in Great Ormond Street Hospital in London and died at the RMC in 2018 at the age of 40, making her the longest lived patient on record with Alexander's Disease. We also had test results from the age of 5 until her death. This, too, is also very unusual.

Another man I saw had Evans Syndrome, a rare autoimmune disorder in which the body makes antibodies that destroy the red blood cells, platelets and white blood cells. People with Evans syndrome may have low levels of all three types of blood cells at one time, or may only have problems with one or two of them. The exact cause of this condition is unknown. There are regular flare-ups of the disorder. This is what happened to the man referred to me. He had been a teacher and spoke several languages but the Evans Syndrome flared up and caused him to have meningitis and a bilateral stroke. He gradually deteriorated over time.

A woman whom we never really understood was referred because she claimed not to have slept for six months. She was British but lived abroad until her husband brought her back to the UK for a diagnosis. I assessed her and found she had some cognitive difficulties. This is part of my neuropsychological assessment report.

> She has significant problems with visual search (Trail making test) where she was very slow.
> She is below average on Digit Span and the RBMT-3.
> She was also slow with her right (dominant) hand on a test of fine motor functioning (the Grooved peg board).

In addition, she has some problems with non-verbal tasks such as matrix reasoning and learning a novel task.

Her verbal skills are generally better. Her naming, her true/false decision making on the speed of comprehension test, and her verbal fluency scores were all normal.

Her social reasoning as assessed by the comprehension sub test on the WAIS-3 was actually well above average (the only subtest where this happened).

I was at a loss, however, to know what her diagnosis was but one possible clue came when Mick and I were at a meeting in Krakow and having lunch with two good friends from Australia, Robyn Tate and Michael Perdices. I was telling them about the patient (with details hidden of course because of confidentiality) when Michael told me about a condition called "Fatal Familial Insomnia" (FFI). As soon as I returned to work I checked up on this and ordered a book about it called *The Family that Couldn't Sleep* (Max, 2006). A Venetian family first developed FFI in the eighteenth century. As the name suggests the condition is incurable and leads to death. People with FFI inherit a tendency to manufacture prions in their own bodies. These accumulate and destroy the brain's sleep centres, resulting in a sweaty, hollow-eyed demented death. A small core of affected individuals lives around Venice. This is the family that couldn't sleep, a key focus of D.T. Max's book. This group of related individuals was shunned until relatively recently because of the strange "curse" that brought death in early middle age to so many of them. The condition is genetic but spontaneous sporadic mutations can occur.

The chief clinical features of FFI include a progressive and ferocious insomnia, waking "sleep", hallucinations, plus autonomic disturbances suggestive of sympathetic overdrive (tachycardia, hypertension, hyperhidrosis, hyperthermia). Unfortunately, before I could arrange for the appropriate genetic testing to be carried out with our patient, her husband had taken her back overseas so we never found out whether or not she had the condition. My guess is that she did not.

One other man we wrote up had Diogenes Syndrome (Ashworth, Rose and Wilson, 2018). This is also known as senile squalor syndrome and is characterised by self-neglect, squalor, withdrawal, apathy and compulsive hoarding. It is associated with several conditions including frontal lobe dementia and learning disability. The condition was first recognised by Clark, Mankikar and Gray (1966). The name derives from Diogenes of Sinope, an ancient Greek philosopher, a cynic and a minimalist who allegedly lived in a barrel. The name is not really appropriate as Diogenes was not a hoarder. When first assessed neuropsychologically, TD was unable to identify emotional expressions of disgust and was borderline-impaired on a facial recognition test. Given he had been living in squalor, neglecting himself and showed little concern for his problems, I was particularly intrigued by his difficulties in identifying expressions of disgust. I was talking about rare and unusual syndromes at a meeting in Maastricht when Fiona Ashworth, listening to the talk, asked questions about TD. She said she was interested in patients who had problems with disgust. This led to Fiona coming to see TD and eventually led to us writing a paper. We questioned whether the basis of his difficulties was neuropsychological or psychological in nature. This became the objective of our study with TD. He completed neuropsychological and psychological assessments alongside an experimental task investigating processing of disgust and his attitudes towards his living situation. We found that when questioned he understood the consequences of living in squalor and could make decisions based on emotions. However, we also found that he had problems identifying smells and showed poor awareness of his own living conditions and showed a lack of shame about them. We believed that both neuropsychological and psychological factors were likely to contribute to his difficulties.

Perhaps the most interesting of these rare and unusual syndromes was described in the paper we wrote about Natasha (Wilson, Rose and Florschutz, 2018) who had been diagnosed with Sheehan's Syndrome (SS). This is a rare condition seen only in women. It is one of the pituitary disorders. The pituitary gland at the base of the brain secretes eight hormones. There is a decrease in the secretion of one or more of these in people with SS. The syndrome is usually caused by a severe loss of blood during or after childbirth leading to decreased functioning of the pituitary gland. The syndrome was named after the British pathologist, Harold Leeming Sheehan, who, in 1937, described a specific association with postpartum shock or haemorrhage and necrosis of the pituitary gland. Although rare in countries with good obstetric care, SS is still frequent in those countries with poor healthcare services. Our patient had developed SS after the birth of her second child. However, she also had sickle cell disease which is not rare and seen primarily in people of African or Caribbean origin as, indeed, was Natasha. People with sickle cell disease often do poorly at school but this was not true of Natasha who had a university degree and a high powered job. When I saw her though she was very severely impaired. In researching SS, I found one of the world experts was a Turkish man, Dr Kelestimur. I emailed him and asked whether sickle cell disease was likely to predispose someone to Sheehan's syndrome, given that it was so rare in the UK. He replied saying he did not know the answer to my question but he did know that she was probably the only person in the world to have *both* SS *and* sickle cell disease and that our client should be written up. This I did with the cooperation of Dr Anita Rose and Dr Gerhard Florschutz.

11 Other happenings

There are many other things I could have included in this book. I will say a little about some of the events which deserve a mention. I won many prizes and honours during my career, the first being the May Davidson award, which I mentioned in Chapter 5. This award was from the BPS – The British Psychological Society (Division of Clinical Psychology) for a major contribution to Clinical Psychology within ten years of qualification. I was made a fellow of the BPS in 1987. From 1996–1998 I was chair of the British Neuropsychological Society, the society that Narinder Kapur and I founded in 1989. One of the biggest awards was an OBE (Order of the British Empire), which I received in the Queen's New Year's Honours list. This is covered in Chapter 6. A number of awards and honours followed, including the Vice-Chair of United Kingdom Acquired Brain Injury Forum in 1998–1999. In 2000 I was awarded The British Psychological Society Award for Distinguished Contributions to Professional Psychology; I became a fellow of the Academy of Medical Sciences in 2001, followed one year later by being voted a fellow of the Academy of Learned Societies for the Social Sciences and the "Professional of the year award" from the Encephalitis support group in 2003. Then in 2004 I won the book of the year award from the BPS for my book, *Case Studies in Neuropsychological Rehabilitation*, which had actually been published in 1999 although the reviews came out later. I was at a meeting of the International Neuropsychological Society in the United States when I heard from the BPS that I had been shortlisted for the award and they needed four copies of the book immediately. I went to Jeffrey House, the American publisher, to tell him and ask for four copies of the book to send to the BPS. He refused! I was shocked as I thought he would see it as an honour. Instead I contacted the British side of the publishing house, Oxford University Press, and the senior man there said he would send four copies straight away to the BPS. I actually won the book of the year award and I hope Jeffrey House felt guilty for not sending four copies of the book. I have received two honorary degrees, one from The University of East Anglia in 2005 and one from the University of Cordoba in Argentina in 2014. I was also the first non-American to win The Robert L Moody Prize for Distinguished Contributions in Brain Injury Rehabilitation and Research. This was given in Galveston, Texas in 2006. I remember that, at the dinner hosted for the award winner and other attendees, I sat next to a man defending capital punishment in the United States. He said, it certainly deterred him from killing! I thought we have not had capital punishment in Great Britain since 1965 and we have a far lower murder rate than the United States. In any case, personal morals should stop one killing others, we do not need capital punishment to prevent killing.

Another thing that happened in 2006 is that a rehabilitation centre in Quito Ecuador was named after me. This was set up by a husband and wife team, Guido Enriquez Bravo and Martha De La Torre. Guido and Martha met me some time earlier at a meeting in South America and asked if they could name their centre after me. I was flattered and agreed. I have visited their centre on two occasions. It is not like the Oliver Zangwill Centre (OZC) partly because most of the patients are children and partly because it is more traditional, having separate physiotherapy, occupational therapy, speech and language therapy and so forth. Thus it is not a holistic centre. On one of my visits though I was asked to speak to the families (through an interpreter) and the problems faced by Ecuadorian families are, unsurprisingly, exactly the same as those faced by British families.

I became president of the International Neuropsychological Society (INS) from 2006–2007. I had been a member of the INS since 1982 and had been on the board. There was another Barbara Wilson active in INS too. She was Barbara C. Wilson and I was Barbara A Wilson. We became friends. She worked with children with language disorders and I worked with adults with memory and other cognitive problems. Confusions regularly arose. Some people thought it was the same person working with children and adults. Once when I gave a talk at an INS meeting, an American asked me why I used British participants! Whenever I checked in at a hotel for the INS meetings I always said that I was the *British* Barbara Wilson not the *American* Barbara Wilson but this did not always stop mistakes from happening. On one occasion a bouquet of flowers was delivered to my room – it was meant for the other Barbara. In Vancouver, I checked in and was sent to a suite which I certainly had not booked. I went back to the reception desk to explain that I had not reserved a suite and that it must be for the other Barbara Wilson. The man said as it was their mistake, I could stay there! Yet another error occurred once when I asked for my key that I had given in earlier and was told that I had checked out! Perhaps the biggest error was when Barbara C. was put up for president. I was on the board then. It was announced at a board meeting that Barbara Wilson had been elected and some of the board members turned to me and clapped. I believe that some of them thought they were voting for me. My turn came later. Mick and I once visited and stayed with Barbara C. and her husband, Jim, in Long Island, New York. They were cat people and had many cats, both indoor cats and outdoor cats. Much of the day was spent preparing food for them all. One of their indoor cats was called Sondra and she was 21 years old. A great age for a cat. Sadly Barbara C. died in 2010 but some people thought I had died and sent condolences to the INS. I liked her a great deal and we often laughed together about the confusion we caused. One of my presidential addresses was entitled "From Models to Muddles" and I started with a photograph of the two Barbara Wilsons saying this was one of the muddles. On another occasion we were both at a meeting in Finland and having a drink with Ed Van Zomeren from the Netherlands. We were all having a good time and Ed said he always wanted to be with two Barbara Wilsons. Barbara and I talked about publishing a paper together written by Barbara Wilson[2] but we never managed to do this and now it is too late.

Also in 2007 I was chosen to be president of the Encephalitis Society and I remain president to this day. In 2010 a group of us trekked in Transylvania, Northern, to collect money for the society. The scenery was stunning but the six-day trek was very demanding. A week before we left, Mick suddenly lost his hearing and his balance was affected. He thought he had an ear infection. I said, well you have to go on this trek as I don't know how to give the money back. I had collected almost £8,000 for the charity. He did go but it was a real struggle for him and he needed help getting up the steep mountainsides. On our return he went to the chemists to ask for something for his ear infection. He was told to go to our doctor's. This he did and was sent to the local hospital, The West Suffolk, the same hospital where I had helped to deliver Francesca. He was eventually diagnosed with an acoustic neuroma! No wonder it was so difficult for him to cope in Transylvania. The West Suffolk sent him to Addenbrooke's, our university teaching hospital in Cambridge, saying that they only saw five patients a year with an acoustic neuroma but Addenbrooke's saw 17 patients a year. We went to Cambridge and had a very good young doctor who explained the options to us. Mick could have surgery, which was hardly ever done by then, or he could have another treatment over several weeks, or we could opt for gamma knife or the most up-to-date treatment, cyber knife. For the last two options Mick had to go to St Bart's in London. We both went up for the appointment and, having listened to the choices, said we would like the cyber knife. This was the most expensive. St Bart's then had to ask our local health authority if they would pay. Given Mick's age this was by no means certain. Fortunately, the local health authority agreed to pay (something in the region of £25,000, which we could not have afforded ourselves). We had to go to St Bart's for three consecutive days for the treatment after a special mask was made for Mick. We stayed in London for two nights and, as Mick had no side effects, we went to museums and art galleries after the treatment. We were also allocated two special nurses, a man and a woman, to answer any questions and provide support. They were both wonderful and we were very grateful that we had a National Health Service. Mick has a regular MRI scan to check on the neuroma but, so far, so good and it stopped growing. His hearing, however, is still poor.

I was Vice President of the Academy for Multidisciplinary Neuro-traumatology from 2007–2010 and have won five lifetime achievement awards: one from the BPS in 2007, one from the INS in 2008, one from The National Academy of Neuropsychology in 2014, one from the Encephalitis Society in 2016 and one from the NHS 70-year anniversary parliamentary awards where I was regional champion for the Midlands and East Region. In 2011, I received the Ramon Y Cahal award from the International Neuropsychiatric Association and, in 2019, I was awarded the annual prize from the Spanish Neuropsychological Society given to an outstanding neuropsychologist. In 2010, the Division of Neuropsychology named a prize after me, the Barbara Wilson prize for outstanding contributions to neuropsychological rehabilitation. This prize has been given every year since then and, in most years, I have been able to give the recipient the award myself. I have three honorary professorships, one from the University of East Anglia, one from the University of Hong Kong and one from the University of Sydney.

One of my favourite meetings is the two-day annual meeting of our Special Interest Group (SIG) in Neuropsychological Rehabilitation. I am chair of that group and have been since we formed in 2006. It actually began in 2001 when I was on sabbatical with Robyn Tate in Sydney. Robyn, Michael Perdices, her husband, and I were visiting a winery in the Hunter Valley and having a wonderful lunch. I spoke about Uluru (also known as Ayers Rock although Uluru is more politically correct). Robyn and Michael said that most Australians did not visit Uluru. I said that we should have a satellite meeting there after the INS in Cairns that would happen in 2004. From then on we started planning for the meeting. We each wrote to everybody we could think of in the neuro rehabilitation world asking them to come to Uluru. We explained they would have to find their own funding and submit an abstract. The meeting happened with 42 participants. The conference dinner was held in the open in the desert and we had a wonderful talk about the stars. It was such a success that we decided to repeat the meeting the following year in Ireland.

The INS was to be held in Dublin and we would hold our meeting in Galway where Agnes was now based. After another successful meeting, we decided to form our own society and I was charged with the task of making sure that there were no other societies we would clash with. As part of my enquiries, I contacted Michael (Mike) Barnes who had set up the World Federation of Neuro Rehabilitation (WFNR). Mike was now an eminent consultant but I had known him when he was a junior registrar working with Lindsay McLellan in Southampton some years before. Mike persuaded me that we should become a special interest group (SIG) of the WFNR. He said we would have secretarial, practical and financial help. I took this idea to our next meeting in Vaduz in Liechtenstein (after the INS in Zurich). The committee agreed that we should join WFNR so that is what we did. Our first formal meeting as part of WFNR was in San Sebastian in Spain in 2007 following the INS meeting in Bilbao. This was followed by meetings in Iguazu Falls, Brazil, Tallin, Estonia, Krakow, Poland, Rotorua, New Zealand, Bergen, Norway, Maastricht, The Netherlands, Limassol, Cyprus, Daydream Island, Australia, Glasgow, Scotland, Cape Town, South Africa, Prague, the Czech Republic and this

Figure 11.1 An ecstatic world explorer, here is Barbara flying over the Namibian desert

summer we go to Granada Spain. We have met in some wonderful parts of the world. I have been chair of the SIG since we began and always give the opening talk. Until recently Robyn Tate was our secretary until she resigned and Michael Perdices took over the post.

In 2012, Volker Homberg, general secretary of the WFNR, appointed me chair of all the SIGs of the WFNR. There are 35 SIGs altogether, and every two years we have a SIG chairs meeting. The first was held in Pavia, Italy and hosted by Caterina Pistarini. The second was held in Abu Dhabi hosted by Sabahat Wasti, the third was in Shanghai in China hosted by Jianan Li and Tieban Yan while the most recent meeting was in Genoa, Italy and hosted once again by Caterina Pistarini. In addition, we have held informal meetings at the WFNR world congresses in Istanbul in 2014, in Philadelphia in 2016 and in Mumbai in 2018. After a general discussion, each SIG has ten minutes to tell the group about their SIG and provide an update over the previous year. WFNR business may also be discussed and possible SIG contributions to the next world congress, which at the time of writing is to be held in Lyon in France in October 2020. Minutes are kept by the WFNR secretary, Tracey Mole. Tracey was Mike Barnes' secretary but when he resigned his leadership of the group Tracey remained as secretary of WFNR. She is the most efficient and competent person and I admire her very much. She lives in the north of England near to Antony Gormley's famous statue, "The Angel of The North". I often say that Tracey Mole is our Angel of The North!

I still like work and continue to go to the OZC regularly and, until May 2019 to The Raphael Hospital one day a week, unless I was abroad. I am not sure, though, for how much longer this will continue as the OZC is under threat because funders are reluctant to pay for our kind of rehabilitation and also because other brain injury rehabilitation centres say they are providing the holistic rehabilitation offered by the OZC. I am not sure this is entirely true but with the financial pressures faced by the NHS and because of the austerity measures placed on us by the Conservative Government, it is almost impossible to secure funding for the patients we specialise in. I was told recently by an NHS manager that the rehabilitation provided by the OZC is a luxury the NHS can no longer afford. The OZC is probably safe for at least one more year. Furthermore, I learned in May 2019 that Dr Gerhard Florschutz had unexpectedly left the Raphael. Immediately, I thought I would be asked to leave as I am an expensive member of staff. The Raphael is now in the hands of an operations manager and a new chief executive officer who is a finance person. I was obviously too costly for the Raphael which appeared to be in financial trouble and, on May 15th, I was asked to leave with one hour's notice! I did not have a contract and worked freelance so the new bosses felt they did not have to give me notice. I could understand this but thought I should have been thanked for the 11 years I worked there, supported the hospital and raised its status. Nor was there a "sorry we have to let you go" or words to that effect. I am not ready to stop work so, in addition to the extra day at the OZC, I am seeing a few private patients (for the first time in my life) and doing some more workshops.

For the last 18 months of working in Kent, Mick drove me to the Raphael. It is 102 miles from our house to the hospital. We left at about 6.10 am and had to go via the notorious Dartford Crossing. On a good day we could do the journey in just under two hours but there was often trouble on the M25 or the M11 or at the crossing itself. The longest time we ever took was six hours when there was a terrible accident on the way. I am a perfectly competent driver but Mick felt it was too much for me to do this long drive and then work for an eight-hour day. We usually stayed at a nearby hotel and returned home the following day. After a few experiments we discovered the Lingfield Marriott Hotel, 16 miles from the Raphael and part of the Lingfield Race Course. We tended to stay there once a week and became friends with some of the staff. In the restaurant where we had dinner, we soon became friends with Michelle, an attentive and helpful waitress. We also knew and liked Martha, originally from Poland, and Sudarka, originally from India. In the mornings when we had breakfast we became friends with Jo, a very friendly woman, who always gave us a kiss. Ray worked part time and often showed us to our table. He used to work for British Airways and travels widely. On the front desk we knew Lauren, Ellie and Constantin. We liked the hotel very much. The rooms are spacious and the views good. We sometimes saw the racing from our room while on other occasions we had views of the golf course. I miss many things about The Raphael Hospital in Kent and Lingfield Marriott hotel but I don't miss the horrible journey.

I used to be seen by some people as a workaholic but I think I have always put family first and I certainly don't work as hard now as I used to. I know that I could not have achieved as much as I have without the support of Mick. He is certainly a modern man despite being born in 1935. We have always shared most of the child rearing and domestic work, I do a little more cooking than him these days and he has always done more housework than me. The family joke is that I don't know how to use the vacuum cleaner (and this is true) but I am a better cook and enjoy trying new recipes and making a meal out of left overs. I almost never waste food and think this stems from the wartime food shortages.

Looking back over this chapter I am a little startled at the number of posts I have held in my professional career and the awards I have received for my clinical work, my research, and my writing. I am certain that my mother would not even comprehend all those titles but it's best not to underestimate the powers of Brixton women perhaps? And I am equally certain that my gender has not been a disadvantage over the years. Familywise I agree that a good man is hard to find but I got lucky with Mick – who is always saying how lucky *he* is!

As I said before, Mick and I attended the National Gatherings of The Compassionate Friends (TCF) regularly in the early years after Sarah died and I took on the role of leader in several discussion groups usually concerned with sudden loss of a child. At the same time Mick started running a creative writing course at these meetings and did so for a period of about ten years. As a result he has collected together an impressive anthology of poems written by parents, mostly mothers, and is hoping to find a publisher willing to take on the daunting business of publishing an anthology of poems written by parents about losing a child. Mick was able to draw on his experience as a teacher in a secondary modern school to encourage members of his writing course to write some powerful and at times beautiful poems, one of which I'd like to quote a little later to give readers an inkling of their depth of feeling and the skill shown by individuals when moved to write about the most tragic loss of a child.

First of all in his sessions, Mick used to discourage rhyming so that members of his class could concentrate on meaning, emotions and the five senses to achieve intensity of expression. He always argued that non-rhyming verse was much more suited to freedom of expression in modern times and that chasing rhymes frequently led to superficiality and doggerel unless the writer was particularly skilled and experienced. Of course, he argued that great writers in the past could write brilliantly in rhyming verse but that nowadays such a medium – unless it is used for song writing, i.e. lyrics, or is an essential part of the new art of rapping, has difficulty in conveying adequately the complexities of modern life.

Mick encouraged his group to write line by line in free verse form, the length of lines differing according to sentence structure, emphasis, rhythm and meaning. Individuals were encouraged to write about their normal, everyday, and even domestic, lives and to show how desperately tragic feelings of loss and pain and anger can crash into that daily existence. They could also try writing as though they were conversing with their lost son or daughter. One of the poets Mick used most frequently for inspiration was Rebecca Goss whose book, *Her Birth* (Carcanet Press, 2013), is a collection of poems about her newborn daughter who lived for 16 months, of which Helen Dunmore writes: "[Rebecca Goss'] poems ... unfold their story of love, loss and grief for a baby daughter with pared down precision and scorching intensity".

Here is one of the poems from Mick's anthology, written by a mother during one of his creative writing sessions:

Just making the gravy

The first Christmas after you died

Alice said "Mum, you don't have to do anything,

we'll do it all – but can you just make the gravy?"

"Of course!" I said.

One small thing. I can manage that.

I managed to make lists

and order food

and buy presents

and wrap them

and dig out the stockings

and decorate the tree

and even send a few cards.

I stood by the hob.

Champagne was being passed around.

Grandchildren were happily weaving

between our legs, clutching presents and chirruping.

I had my apron on, ready.

Alice took the turkey out of the oven,

and put the roasting tin down in front of me.

"Mum, can you just make the gravy?

That's all you have to do."

That's all I have to do.

But – I – can't

I cannot move. I cannot lift my arm.

I'm standing in front of the turkey,

paralysed

with tears pouring down my cheeks.

The first Christmas without you

I could not even manage the gravy.

For Chloe, who died on 4th August, 2009, aged 37.
By Jill Yglesias

12 Family and friends

From the moment I married I wanted a baby and was fortunate to become pregnant with Sarah very quickly. She was born 11 months after we married. Anna arrived 15 months later and Matthew 18 months after that. Sarah was born by caesarean section. She was an eight pound baby and I am only five foot tall so the doctors were worried that my pelvis was small. The real problem though was that they made me stay in bed during labour while my body knew it needed to keep moving. The baby was fine but I knew that with the second baby I would not go to the hospital until much later. I was actually booked for a C-section on September 14th but went into labour on the night of September 12th. I walked around our flat all night. I knew it was important to keep moving. In the morning Mick and I put Sarah in the pram and walked about two miles to Lexden Maternity Home (which no longer exists). Every time I had a contraction I had to stop to pee (behind a bush if possible). We arrived at the maternity home, and Mick left as he had to take Sarah to a nursery we had found to look after her while I was in hospital and Mick went to work. Soon afterwards the baby was ready to come. A wonderful midwife talked me through and told me when to push and when to stop pushing and Anna was born very easily on September 13th. Hers was definitely the best birth of my three children and I didn't need the planned C-section after all. Because her birth was so straightforward I was allowed a home birth with Matthew. His birth was not quite as easy. During one of the contractions, his heart stopped so the midwife called the family doctor, Dr Steeds, whom I was a little in love with. He didn't know what to do, I am sure midwives know more than doctors and, in any case, the baby's heart had started again. I remember shouting during labour saying "all this bloody wasted hard work" as it was such an effort, but the baby arrived without much trouble and Mick came in at the last moment. This was in 1966 just before fathers were encouraged to be present at births.

Matthew was almost a cot death at a few weeks old; he almost drowned in a paddling pool when he was a few months old and he fell on a fence which went through his leg when he was about 4 years old. He also came down a slide and just missed a piece of glass at the bottom. Talk about accident prone – he was constantly at the hospital but somehow he survived all this. Anna was the least trouble – she slept a great deal and probably missed out on some attention. Sarah cried every time I put her down so I carried her everywhere for months. Matthew demanded attention but Anna, the middle babe, was left more than she should have been. A school doctor once asked how Sarah got a bruise on her leg. I didn't know so I asked Sarah how it happened. She couldn't remember but the doctor said not to worry. In retrospect, I think she was checking for non-accidental injury but the fact that I asked Sarah meant I wasn't trying to cover anything up. Anna did give us one scare. On her first day at school she fell and bumped her head in the playground and was taken to hospital for observation. She was fine, however. I knew Sarah was a clever girl and realised Anna was too when her teacher at primary school told me not to underestimate her. I think she realised she was in danger of being overlooked because of her big sister and her younger brother. Anna did best of all at school and university. She is now a clinical psychologist and a successful woman.

We thought the children had a wonderful childhood. We lived on the outskirts of Reading and Mick often took the children over to Sulham Woods and formed the Red Fox Gang. Cindy, Sarah's best friend joined the gang and sometimes Nicola, Anna's friend, came too. I was typically working at this stage. I don't think Anna feels so good about her childhood as Sarah and Matthew.

Both girls married and both divorced. Anna's first husband was Paul, the father of Rosie, and Sarah married Gez. Anna and Paul split up when Rosie was 4 and Anna renewed her acquaintance with Dennis, who was the father of Francesca. Rosie and Paul are still in contact but Francesca's father died. Anna and Dennis never married but Anna is now happily married to Mike, a structural engineer. Both are grandparents, Mike's daughter has two little boys and Rosie has Amelie, our great granddaughter.

We feel privileged to be alive and well with a great granddaughter who fills us with delight. I have already mentioned Matthew's marriage to Andrea. They live in Chile in one of the wine-growing areas two hours' drive south of Santiago. They have two handsome and clever

Figure 12.1 We do have a selfie! Females from four generations of the Wilson Family. [From left to right] Barbara, mother, grandmother and great grandmother; Anna, daughter; Amelie, great granddaughter; Rosie and Francesca, granddaughters

sons, Sammy and Max. They are, of course, bilingual, which makes me proud. The sad thing is that Sarah will never know these boys and they will never know Sarah, although they know all about her and talk about her frequently. We love our children, grandchildren and great granddaughter. We have a wonderful life apart from that one terrible tragedy, which is part of who we are. We still feel Sarah is part of our family; we wonder what life would be like if she had lived. We would never have known The Compassionate Friends; we would never have found it so easy to talk about death and bereavement; we would never have made an immediate bond with other bereaved parents and would probably have been more selfish. Sarah's death has, I believe, made us better people although we were not bad people to begin with.

Most of my friends are known through work and I have referred to some of them in previous texts. One of my dearest friends is Jill Winegardner, an American citizen who worked for several years at the Oliver Zangwill Centre (OZC). I first met Jill in 1986 at a meeting of the International Neuropsychological Society (INS) in Veldhoven, near

Eindhoven in The Netherlands. Muriel Lezak, a famous neuropsychologist, introduced us over lunch. She said that she thought Jill and I would get on with each other. We did, and have been friends ever since. Jill is one of the bravest people I know. She came from a banking family in Montana but when I knew her she worked in brain injury rehabilitation in Cleveland, Ohio. I say she is brave because she once worked for several years in Nicaragua to teach neuropsychology as well as to support the Sandinista revolution that was under attack by the US government at the time. Jill first went to Nicaragua for eight weeks in the autumn of 1988 to teach a six-week course on neuropsychology (with Tedd Judd) to a group of professional psychologists in Managua through the Nicaraguan Psychological Association. It was the first formal offering of neuropsychology teaching in the country. Jill and Tedd founded the Association of Neuropsychology in Nicaragua and Jill is a lifelong founding member.

She then returned to Managua in October 1990 and stayed there until around March 1993. She worked through the Association of Neuropsychology in Nicaragua and taught neuropsychology at the National Rehabilitation Hospital, supervised theses of psychology students at the University of Central America, provided clinical supervision to a select group of psychologists working in a variety of clinical settings in Managua, and wrote a practical manual on neuropsychology for use in Spanish-speaking countries. Jill goes back every year as a founding member of the Central American Women's fund and to look after her project, Terrabona Health, that supports rural health care.

While in Nicaragua, Jill lived with the poor people there. She speaks fluent Spanish, which she taught herself because of going to live in Managua. She has driven herself from Cleveland to Managua several times – so all through the United States, Mexico, Guatemala, El Salvador, and Honduras. She is a very political and sensible person who is totally admirable. Jill left the United States to work for the British NHS. She became a British citizen and Mick and I went to the low-key but rather sweet ceremony. However, the United States tempted her back and she returned there in November 2018. We are still hoping she will come back to the UK.

Another good friend is Jessica Fish. In fact, I call her my "adopted daughter" and she feels like a daughter to me. Jessica is clever, modest, helpful and a huge support. I first met her when she came to Cambridge as a summer student in 2003. I agreed to take a summer student and had to look through an enormous pile of applications. I didn't know where to start but as I was leafing through I saw the name Huw Williams. I knew Huw, he used to work at the OZC. He was listed as the referee for Jessica Fish. I telephoned him and mentioned Jessica and said, "Is she good and would she fit in with the team here in Cambridge?" Huw replied "Yes and yes," so I offered Jessica the placement. She was a success and came back the following year to pursue another placement with a colleague. Then after graduation she applied to do a PhD at the MRC unit (the PhD studentships are affiliated to Cambridge University). She was successful and was jointly supervised by Tom Manly and myself. I always felt that Jessica should complete her clinical training as we wanted people like her in the profession. Initially, however, she was tired of being a student and wanted a job so she took a post doc position at the MRC unit in Cambridge. After a spell of this, she did complete her clinical training at the Institute of Psychiatry in London (where I had trained years earlier). Eventually Jessica came to work at the OZC and was a colleague until September 2018 when she moved to work with Shai Betteridge, another friend of mine, who is head of psychology at St Georges Hospital in London. Before saying more about Shai, I want to say that Jessica is now editor of *The Neuropsychologist* and an excellent clinical psychologist both clinically and research wise. To illustrate Jessica's helpfulness, when I was writing my book *Memory Rehabilitation: Integrating Theory and Practice* (published in 2009), I was very bad about chasing up references and didn't write them down as I went along. When it came to the reference section I found myself in a real muddle and said to Jessica that I thought I was going mad. She said she would help and she did, finding all the references for me. To this day when I get stuck with a reference or if I am not sure how to cite something I found online, Jessica helps me out. She is an absolute treasure.

I have great admiration for another friend and colleague, Shai Betteridge. She is a phenomenal worker who gets by on very little sleep and has great ideas about neuropsychological rehabilitation. My first memory of Shai is when she asked if I would provide supervision for her when I was at the OZC before retirement. I didn't think I would be very good as I am out of date with CBT and emotional or mood issues but Shai said I was just right for the neuro rehabilitation aspects so we met a few times at the OZC. Apparently, we had met before, according to Shai, but my memory dates from the supervision days at the OZC. Shai was then promoted to her present job and we kept in touch. Some time later we were at a meeting together and I said that I wanted to go to Rwanda on a gorilla trek but could not find anyone to go with me. Shai said she would come! We organised the trip and went to Rwanda in 2012. I have been on many safaris but never to see gorillas. Shai had never been to Africa before. We had the most amazing trip and spent two days in Virunga National Park. We were allocated to two different gorilla families. Eight people are in a group with the guides and trackers. Each group is allocated to one of the habituated gorilla families and when the group reaches their allotted family it can stay observing the family for one hour. The trackers know where each family is but our first family had moved across a mountain so we had a very difficult trek to get to the group. When we finally arrived, the family had finished feeding; the adults were mostly resting while the youngsters were playing. We had been told how to behave. There was a wonderful huge male silverback a few feet from us. I fell in love at first sight. The second family we saw, a few days later, was much easier to find and was still feeding when we arrived. Both families were enthralling to watch but I will never forget that first silverback who won my heart. We had seen some golden monkeys in between times, but after the gorillas they were a bit of a disappointment. We also saw the genocide museum in Rwanda's capital, Kigali, which was harrowing and sombre. From Rwanda we flew to Kenya and went on a trip to a game reserve near the city. Shai saw most of the big five (the iconic safari animals) and thought she was lucky to see so much on her first African trip. Our final visit in Nairobi was to the David Sheldrick elephant orphanage. I didn't want to go because I found it so sad that these babies were orphaned because of poaching. We were persuaded to go, however, and I was impressed with the care the baby elephants received and the trust they had in the keepers.

On another trip to Africa in 2017, Shai and I went to see aardvark. On my extensive safari experiences, I had never seen an aardvark and this was high on my list of animals I wanted to see. We were both at an INS meeting in Cape Town followed by a rehabilitation meeting there too. I told Shai that I wanted to see an aardvark and had found a trip specialising in finding these creatures. Again Shai said she would come even though it would not be a typical safari trip. We flew to Pretoria after the conferences in order to drive to Karoo for our safari. On the aeroplane I was telling Shai about a book I was then writing for Guilford Press, *Essentials of Neuropsychological Rehabilitation*. Shai made several suggestions and I realised that the book would be enhanced if we were to write it together. This came to pass and the book is now published (Wilson and Betteridge, 2019). Meanwhile we continued our journey. We actually saw two aardvark, at pretty close quarters. They were much bigger than I expected. Two Americans staying at the same lodge as us worked for the United Nations. We had had the referendum the year before and I asked the Americans what they thought about the result. "Suicidal," they said and we agreed with them. Mick and I have been on marches, filled in petitions and tried hard to stop this stupid Brexit idea, but at the moment it is still not clear just what is going to happen.

Another colleague and friend whom I like and admire is Jonathan (Jon) Evans. I have mentioned him several times already. He is one of the most liked and respected neuropsychologists in the UK and, indeed, in much of the world. I feel he is my "adopted son". I feel that Jon is my successor and will be even more of a leading light in neuropsychological rehabilitation than he is already.

My other "adopted daughter" is Anita Taub in Brazil. On my frequent trips to Brazil, I stay with Anita and have my own room in her house. I have known Anita for a long time, she knew Sarah too. We met in about 1996 when I was giving a lecture in Brazil. In 1998 Sarah and I were both back there, I was giving a workshop and Sarah was exhibiting tests and books for her father's publishing company. We were at one of the airports in Sao Paulo when we heard someone calling "Dr Barbara, Dr Barbara." It was Anita Taub telling us we were at the wrong airport. We were supposed to be met at the other airport. Anita explained that she was seeing her boyfriend off so could not come with us and we should get a taxi to the hotel. This we did and it all worked out well. The one and a half day workshop finished at lunchtime on Mother's Day in Brazil. Anita asked what we were going to do for Mother's Day. It wasn't important for us so we said we would go back to the hotel and maybe do some shopping. "You can't do that on Mother's Day" said Anita, "you must come to my mother's." She phoned her mother to check it was OK and we accompanied her to her mother's house. This was a very special occasion; we found ourselves embraced by a large Jewish family ranging in age from the 90-year-old grandmother who came originally from Russia, to a 2-year-old boy. Everyone spoke English, we were warmly welcomed and had a wonderful time. Anita and I have been friends ever since.

Her mother offered to help when Sarah died in Peru, we visited Anita and her then boyfriend, Pascal, at his home on St Bart's in The Caribbean and stayed with her mother in her country house at Campo St George in Brazil. This happened a year or two after Sarah died. We stayed at the beautiful house in a small town that reminded us of Switzerland. We were told that there was a music festival in town at the time and one of the neighbours had an auditorium where there was a rehearsal taking place. Would we like to go? We said we would and went to the rehearsal. There was a Russian pianist, a Japanese flautist, a German player and other musicians of different nationalities. It was fascinating. At the end I said to the Japanese flautist that we had a French friend who was a flautist. We were asked his name and we said "Jean Ferrandis", to which the Japanese musician replied, "He is one of my best friends!" What a small world!

Who would have thought that in a town resembling Switzerland in a far corner of Brazil we would meet someone who would know Jean Ferrandis, a man we had known since he was a young child.

Anita Taub also persuaded us to go to Fernando de Noronha, a group of islands off the coast of Brazil and a UNESCO world heritage site. We stayed with a family there, as there were no hotels at that time. One day the father said he was taking his family out on their boat and invited us to join them. We did, it was a glorious day, the father fished and cooked the fish on the boat for lunch. They tasted divine and we were in heaven. Another day we were walking on a cliff and, looking down into the bay, we saw about 300 dolphins. Fernando de Noronha is a very special place. Much of Brazil is. We have been to The Amazon twice, the Pantanal, a huge wildlife area, Salvador, a stunning city, Brasilia, interesting for its architecture and other places. Some of the best restaurants are in Brazil, especially in Sao Paulo. I have other good friends in Brazil and I am co-chair of the Brazilian special interest group in neuropsychological rehabilitation. Two other special Brazilian friends are Fabricia Loschiavo Alvares from Belo Horizonte and Eliane Miotto from the University of Sao Paulo.

I was once hospitalised in Brazil in a town called Goiania. It happened like this. Mick and I had just returned from Oman where, among other things, we spent a night in the deserted desert, the empty quarter it is called and, of course, we had a guide with us. We returned home on an overnight flight and I went straight from the airport to the doctor's to get my annual injection against influenza, which I have had for a number of years with no ill effect. I wanted to get the flu jab quickly as I was due to go to Goiania in four days. That afternoon we went to Anna's and I started to feel ill. I went home to sleep thinking I would feel better soon. I am rarely ill and wasn't too worried. However, I felt very unwell the following day too and could not stay awake. I was sleeping for 20 hours out of 24. I thought I must have had a bad reaction to the flu jab and phoned Dr Rutherford, our very good GP. She said she had not heard of this reaction but would find out for me. She phoned me later to say that occasionally this happened. Was I getting night sweats? I said yes that this was happening. Dr Rutherford said that it should clear up in a few days. I was too unwell to go to the OZC and telephoned Andrew the manager to call in sick. I had not had any sick leave in 27 years so I hated breaking my record but I was really ill. I did not want to cancel the trip to Brazil as I had bought the tickets, promised to go and, in any case kept thinking I would be all right the following day. Mick drove me to Heathrow for the overnight flight to Sao Paulo. I slept in the lounge and slept throughout the flight. The next day I had to get from the international terminal to the domestic terminal to fly to Goiania. I was so ill and felt dreadful. I finally got to Goiania, made it to the hotel and slept for 7 hours. When I woke, my night clothes were so wet with sweat I threw them away, as the thought of washing them nauseated me. I could not eat and just wanted to sleep. Mick was in touch via email and was worried about me. He made me promise to tell the organisers that I needed to see a doctor. I did the first talk with my head buzzing and resting my back against the lectern. At the end of the talk, I said to the main organiser that I had to see a doctor or go to the hospital as I was seriously ill. She took me to the local hospital and one of the senior doctors there spoke English. He arranged an x-ray and came back later to say I had a lower right lung pneumonia and had to stay in the hospital. I said I couldn't as I had another talk to give the next day and in three days' time I was going to Chile. He told me that I might not get to Chile. at which point I started to cry saying I had family there and they would look after me.

The doctor then persuaded me to stay in the hospital for 24 hours. I had a drip in my arm and was put on strong antibiotics. I was taken to a room and the organiser made a young woman who spoke English stay with me to translate! This poor young woman had to sleep on the floor! I said to the organiser, I think her name was Sandra, that I would pay the cost with my credit card and claim it back with insurance when I arrived home. "No, no, no," she said. "We will pay." That was a good surprise. After 24 hours, I was beginning to feel a little better and was allowed back to the hotel. The doctor asked me the time of my flight to Chile. I said it was at 11.30 am. He said the x-ray department opened at 8.30 am. I was to go to the hospital then to have an x-ray and if the pneumonia had shrunk I could go to Chile – if not, I had to stay in Goiania. On arrival at the hotel, I promptly fell asleep again. I had missed my second talk but I was on the mend. On Monday morning at 8.30 am I went back for my x-ray. The pneumonia had shrunk and I was allowed to fly to Chile. I had a letter to give to my doctor back home and a copy of the x-ray. The young woman with good English was made to fly from Goiania to Sao Paulo with me to make sure I checked in OK and caught the right flight. I said to Sandra that she didn't need to do this as I was definitely feeling better. I added that this would not happen in England. Sandra answered "But we are Brazilian!" I was very impressed with the treatment I received in Brazil. I made it to Chile and Matthew met me in Santiago. He gasped when he first saw me as I did not look my usual healthy self. After two days I had to return to Santiago to give five talks at a conference there. I managed, but slept in between talks and did not really return to full health until after I returned home.

Two very good friends that I have mentioned before are Robyn Tate and her husband, Michael Perdices from Sydney, Australia. Michael was born in Spain and moved to Australia at the age of 12 years. I have completed a sabbatical with Robyn in Sydney and she has completed a sabbatical with me in Cambridge. The four of us get on well together and one of our best ever holidays was with Robyn and Michael in Mallorca in 2018. Despite being Spanish, Michael had never been to the island. Mick and I love it and find the island beautiful, sophisticated and very varied, although, of course, we avoid the places where the drunken Brits go, such as Magaluf. We love the weather, the people, the food, the wine and the beauty of much of Mallorca. We wanted to show Robyn and Michael the island we love. We started in Castell Son Claret, one of the leading hotels of the world near Andratx, followed by three days at our timeshare in Son Antem, a Marriott resort (which we own two weeks a year) and then three days at Cap Rocat, a converted fort and one of our favourite hotels anywhere in the world. We had a wonderful time, excellent food, we visited Robert Graves' house, a particular favourite of Robyn's, and were sad to separate in order for Robyn and Michael to return to Madrid and us to return to the UK.

I have strong links with South America, Sarah died there, Matt, Andrea, Sammy and Max live there, one of my "adopted" daughters, Anita Taub, lives there. I have an honorary degree from the University of Cordoba in Argentina, thanks to the very helpful and likeable Andrea Querejeta and I have other good friends and colleagues in Buenos Aires: namely Facundo Manes, Teresa Torralva and Natalia Sierra. Other good friends are in India, another country I have visited several times. I would like to mention Urvashi Shah from Mumbai, Aparna Dutt from Kolkata, Jwala Narayanan from Bangalore, Farzana Mulla from Pune and Nithya Hariya Mohan from Chennai. All these people and more have made my trips to India so rewarding. As I have said to friends and colleagues on several occasions, India is both awful and wonderful at the same time but the wonderful bits outweigh the awful bits and everyone should visit India. The hospitality is excellent and there are so many treasures to see. My good friend Narinder Kapur is a British Indian who left India when he was 2 years old and grew up in Northern Ireland. Narinder still has strong links with India and has been at the same meetings as me on many occasions. He regularly donates to Indian charities and is a very moral man who is a supporter of Gandhi. My father always supported Gandhi against the British Government when I was a young child so Gandhi is one of my heroes too along with Aneurin Bevan who was responsible for creating the NHS.

13 More about travels

I have been to many countries and call myself a serious traveller. I often travel for work but also for pleasure. I have travelled extensively for conferences, lectures and workshops in Europe, South America and North America and less extensively in Australia, New Zealand, Africa and Asia. I have been to meetings in countries considered by some to be dangerous such as Lebanon, Nigeria and Iran. In all these countries I have been treated well and liked the people very much. In Lebanon, we were taken to visit Byblos (from where we get the word "Bible") a beautiful city on the coast. The host in Lebanon was Dr Fadi Abou-Mrad who has organised some good neuropsychology meetings. I was once at a lunch in Lebanon, where, by the way, the food is exceptionally good, and I found myself talking to a woman from the Druze community. We were talking about treating people in groups and I said I was a bereaved mother then mentioned the support I had received from the group The Compassionate Friends. We went on to visit a historical site and, while there, the Druze woman came up to me to tell me she was a bereaved parent who had lost her baby son 20 years ago. Apart from to her sister she had never talked about the loss. We hugged as bereaved parents tend to do and felt a strong bond with each other. I thought how easy it was to make a rapport with a woman from a different country, a different religion, a different language but with one powerful connection between us, the loss of a child. Truly our similarities as humans are far greater than our differences. As I write these words on May 12th 2019, it is the nineteenth anniversary of Sarah's death. Jon Evans sent an email saying he was thinking of us. He always remembers every year, the only person outside the family to do this. Pleased at Jon's gesture, his words made me cry, nevertheless.

Nigeria is another country many British people are frightened to go to but again the hospitality was great. My main difficulty with Nigeria was obtaining the visa to get there in the first place. The meeting was scheduled for early December 2018. I needed my passport for travel to Alicante in November so had about ten days to organise the visa. The website said it would take a week to obtain a visa. I went onto the website one Saturday morning and found I first had to register my credit card – I could not just use the card to pay the fee. I had to scan in a credit card bill to prove I was the person I claimed to be. By the time I had worked out how to do that several hours had passed. I then had to apply for a visa and arrange an appointment with the Nigerian Embassy in London. I completed the form and tried to submit but a message came back saying my home address was wrong! I certainly know my home address! I kept trying to submit the form for most of the day on Sunday – using capital letters, lower case letters, spaces in and out, in fact every variation I could think of but each time I was told my home address was wrong. I was in tears and ready to cancel the whole trip but decided to ask for help from one of the administration staff at the Oliver Zangwill Centre (OZC) the following day, before abandoning the effort. Next morning, at the OZC, I asked Rachel Everett for help. She is good with computers and technology. At first Rachel had the same trouble as me, before reading everything carefully and telling me that my credit card form was too big! She shrank it and all went through fine. It was nothing to do with my home address at all. Then Rachel arranged an appointment for me in London. I went on the train the following day, taking all the papers I thought I needed. After a wait in the offices, I was called to see the man dealing with visas and gave him all my paperwork. He then asked me for my bank statement to show I had enough money to support myself. It had not said on the website that I needed a bank statement so I began to panic a little. I told the man I had online banking and could show him my current account on my iPad. He said that was not good enough and I had to have a printed statement to send off with everything else. He asked where I banked and I said NatWest. He told me there was a NatWest across the road and I could get a statement printed there. I went to the bank and it was obvious that I was not the first person needing such a statement. The man there knew exactly what was required and provided the statement quickly. I went back to the Nigerian Offices and after a shorter wait gave everything required and was told that all being well I could come back a week later to collect the visa. Relieved, I made my way back to Kings Cross to take the train to Cambridge and then to make the connection to Bury St Edmunds. That was not the end of my troubles though, as once on the train I went to put a note in my Filofax to remind me to do something and realised I had left my Filofax in the embassy offices! I was on the mainline train so could not go back to the embassy. On my return home I phoned the embassy but could not get through. I was able to phone the next day and eventually spoke to someone who said she would look in lost property. She telephoned later to say the Filofax was not there. I felt so low, I had all my appointments in there plus notes from the past 20 years and all sorts of important information. I changed all my passwords, bought another Filofax and tried to reconstruct everything. I continued to feel bad about the lost Filofax but at least the visa was ready after one week. I went on the train again to London to collect the visa and as I was leaving I mentioned to the man that the previous week I had left a Filofax there. He said I should speak to the security man. I asked if that was the man who checked us in at the front desk and was told it was. So, on my way out, I told the security man about my lost Filofax. He said he had seen it, retrieved it for me and I was reunited with the treasured Filofax. What a palaver to get a visa to go to a country for four days! I have become frustrated at getting visas for India, Russia and China but none of these was as bad as obtaining a visa for Nigeria. It was an interesting visit though and wonderful in some ways but chaotic in others.

One of the most remarkable trips and the one with far-seeing consequences was to Iran. This happened when I met Dr Hamed Ekhtiari at a meeting in Istanbul, Turkey in 2014. He heard me talk and then invited me to lunch. I asked if Jill could come too. We went together and were asked if we would be willing to go to Iran to give a workshop. We both thought how interesting this would be, accepted the invitation and went to Iran in April 2015 to give a four-day workshop and two lectures. Dr Hamed Ekhtiari is a medical doctor and a cognitive neuroscientist from Tehran, the capital of Iran, who was able to obtain a government grant to cover our costs. We left London Heathrow on Thursday April 2nd to fly to Istanbul where we had to spend two nights in order to collect our visas for Iran. On Saturday April 4th we left Istanbul for Tehran arriving late at night. Before disembarking we had to make sure we were appropriately dressed. This meant no bare arms or legs, loose clothing from neck to knees, and scarves over our heads and covering our necks. After some questioning at immigration, we were allowed through and met by two of our hosts, Tara Rezapour and Fatemeh Mosavi, who took us to the Parsian Azadi Hotel, one of the largest in Tehran. The following day began with a short meeting about the week with Dr Ekhtiari, and then sightseeing. I shook hands with Dr Ekhtari before Tara took me quietly aside to say that men and women did not shake hands!

The workshop took place at one of Tehran's hospitals. We had about 50 participants, many of them students at Tehran universities who were studying cognitive rehabilitation, and a fair number of occupational therapists (OTs) including some lecturers in OT from the university. Jill and I shared the talks and the workshop exercises, covering general principles of: neuropsychological rehabilitation; assessment; and strategies for managing attention, memory, executive, perceptual, behavioural and social communication problems. The audience was very engaged, many questions were asked and our style was appreciated. We presented the views of the Oliver Zangwill Centre, stressing that rehabilitation should be holistic, a partnership of professionals and family, and should address not only cognitive, but also emotional and psychosocial issues. We criticised computer-based cognitive training exercises because of lack of evidence and emphasised the need to evaluate and seek evidence for the efficacy of rehabilitation. Each lunchtime and evening, different participants shared the meal times with us in order to discuss their studies and learn from our visit.

On Friday morning we rose very early to fly to Shiraz, Iran's sixth largest city. This is where Shiraz wine originally came from although, of course, alcohol is now forbidden in Iran (the earliest wine in the world came from Shiraz 7,000 years ago!). After leaving our overnight bags at the lovely Hotel Shiraz, where we were to spend Friday night, we drove 70 kilometres to Persepolis, city of the ancient Persians, and a UNESCO world heritage site. It was splendid but very hot and difficult for the women, who had to be covered up so much. The men were allowed to be far more casual, wearing shorts and T-shirts if they wished. In the afternoon, we visited some beautiful gardens and the tombs of two of Iran's famous poets.

On Saturday lunchtime, we gave a talk on Cognitive Rehabilitation at Shiraz University. Most of the participants there were physiotherapists and less interested than those in Tehran. After a late lunch we returned to the airport to fly back to Tehran. Shiraz is a more beautiful city with less traffic than Tehran. However, the snow-capped mountains surrounding Tehran were lovely.

Sunday was a busy day. We gave a lecture at the university first and felt that went well. This was followed by a discussion about the future of rehabilitation in Iran. Some very eminent people were there and a lively discussion took place. We felt that we were in at the beginning of rehabilitation services in Iran and had, hopefully, provided some ground rules on the way to ensure good rehabilitation practices. The day ended with a final discussion with four senior members of the Strategic Council of Foreign Relations chaired by the president, Kamal Kharrazi, who used to be Foreign Minister in the Iranian government and had worked with Robin Cook and Jack Straw from the Labour Party. We left for home very early the next morning.

The visit was certainly interesting and worthwhile. The people we met were wonderful. So many of them welcomed us to their country and said they hoped we would be happy there, and even some strangers on the street wanted their photographs taken with us. We were treated extremely well and the hospitality was exceptionally good. We realised how difficult it is for the Iranians, because of the sanctions, to access books and tests (they cannot, for example, order anything from Amazon or purchase neuropsychological tests from the international test companies). They are educated people with a very low rate of illiteracy and want to do the best for their country. Our only complaint was that we had to wear the same dress code as the locals even though we are from a different culture. Jill and I never talk about clothes at home yet much of our conversation in our hotel room was about what to wear and whether our outfits were appropriate. Nevertheless, we were grateful for our experience and left Iran with feelings of admiration for the enthusiasm and intelligence of the professionals we met, and look forward to Iran developing excellent neuropsychological rehabilitation. Dr Hamed Ekhtiari, Tara Rezapour, Fatemeh Mosavi and Jamal Hameshi made our visit so special. We found the people to be educated and intelligent with good English. One of the women I liked particularly was a senior lecturer in OT at the university. I felt she agreed with our complaints about the dress code. I asked her once what the women did when it became really hot. "We suffer," she replied. I asked if they ever fainted with the heat and she agreed that sometimes the women did. Just to add one extra note, Jill and I were so fed up with the dress code, we complained about it regularly. The Iranians tended to agree with us. One night in one of the restaurants we decided to stage a little rebellion. The Iranian women, Jill and I, with the approval of the Iranian men present, took off our headscarves and showed our hair. A few minutes later, the owner of the restaurant went up to Dr Ekhtari and asked him to ask us to cover our heads as he thought the police were around. Jill and I were prepared to fight our own corner but we did not want to get our hosts into trouble so we covered our heads again.

Before I went to Iran, Mick asked me to look out for a Persian carpet. We had a second-hand one at home that we bought from an Iranian (a Persian man) selling carpets in Bury St Edmunds. Of course, I could not use a credit card and did not have sufficient local cash so thought it would be impossible for me to purchase a carpet, but one evening before dinner we all went into a carpet shop to look. I said to the owner that I simply wanted to look as I had no money and could not use a credit card. The man asked me where I lived and when I told him I lived in England, he said his brother lived in Liverpool and I could pay him when I arrived home! I was rather astounded at this but decided to go ahead to purchase a carpet. Jill and I looked carefully and chose a lovely red carpet with a separate note about how it was made. I asked the man if he could ship it but it was too difficult to arrange the shipping. Then Jill said that we could manage it ourselves. We bought a cloth holdall and managed to pack the bag in that and bring it back to the UK where it is now in our sitting room. I sent the money to the brother in Liverpool immediately.

The trip to Iran was in April 2015, I went to the United States again in 2015 after the trip to Iran with no trouble, but I had a different experience in December 2016 when I was invited to give a lecture at the Kessler Foundation in New Jersey. I arrived at Newark and went to the man at immigration, a procedure I was very familiar with. He took ages looking at my passport, with the man behind me in the queue looking frustrated. Eventually, the immigration officer said, "Why were you in Iran?" I laughed and said that I was giving a workshop. He then said, "Well you are coming with me. ma'am," and led me to an office at the back where I was detained with other "suspicious" people! After some time, I was called in to be interviewed by two officers; it was a "good cop, bad cop" situation. I was asked why I was in Iran, when I went, did I have dual nationality, did I use Facebook and so on. I was told that they did not understand the Arabic in my visa, which was in the passport. I wanted to say that the Iranians don't speak Arabic, they speak Farsi but I did not say that as I thought they would think I was cocky. They said that anyone who had been to any of five countries (it is now seven) including Iran, in the last five years was questioned on entering the United States. I asked what would happen, thinking I would be sent home, and wondered about the lecture I was scheduled to give at The Kessler Foundation. The men, who obviously realised I was not a terrorist, said I would be given a temporary visa. "How long will that take?", I said. The reply was "not long". I found that unhelpful and was very fed up by this stage. I thought I have been president of The International Neuropsychological Society, which is largely composed of Americans, I was the only non-American to receive the lifetime achievement award from The National Academy of Neuropsychology (an American Organisation) and the first non-American to receive the Robert Moody award. I went to Iran to help them with their brain injury services and now I have been subjected to this interrogation. I felt that I never wanted to go to the United States again but I had already purchased a ticket to New Orleans for February 2018 to go to an INS meeting. In fact it was the fiftieth birthday of INS and several ex-presidents, including me, were being interviewed and filmed for the archives. I explained this and was told I would have to be interviewed at the American Embassy in London to obtain a full visa and would never more be allowed into the United States on the visa waiver scheme.

I sat in the waiting room until my temporary visa was ready and realised the driver waiting outside to take me to the hotel near The

Kessler Foundation would think I wasn't coming, so I went to the guy at the desk and said, "Excuse me, Sir." I never use the word "Sir" as it is not something Brits do, especially rebellious Brits like me, but I was trying to persuade the man to be helpful. "Excuse me, Sir, but I have a driver waiting outside, can I make a phone call?" The man very rudely said "No, you can't." I thought he might say, "I'm sorry that's not allowed" or "Unfortunately, you can't." I did not expect rudeness. I sat down again wondering how I was going to get to the hotel. Just then the "good cop" from the interview walked past and I explained to him that I needed to contact the driver, would he use my phone to make the call? He agreed and the driver waited. Meanwhile I waited and waited, until a man came in waving a piece of paper and calling out my name. I went up to him and he gave me the temporary visa saying he had filled it in all by himself and had saved me 400 dollars! He sounded like a child! I thought I hope he is not expecting a tip as I might be done for bribery. Needless to say the Americans I met later were horrified by the story. This happened at a time when Donald Trump had been voted in but not yet inaugurated. I suspect the reason I was allowed in previously, even though I had been to Iran, was that Trump had not been voted in – either that or the immigration people had not checked my passport thoroughly. I have been told since that immigration at Newark is particularly difficult. I had not saved the 400 dollars either as when I returned and set up the meeting at the American Embassy in London, I must have spent about £500 getting the interview, paying for the visa and then collecting the visa.

The visit to The Kessler was successful and I returned home, still appalled at my treatment at immigration. I set up the interview with the American Embassy in London, online and chose a time. I expected I would be seen close to that time but that was not to be. I went by train to London and made my way to the American Embassy. There was a huge queue outside the embassy, everyone in the line had been given the same time. We waited there for a long time and I met all sorts of interesting people trying to get a visa to go to the United States. Eventually we started to move and went through security. Then we sat in a big hall. My name was called fairly early and I thought that was not so bad but that call was just to make sure I had taken the correct documents with me. I was asked to wait again and this seemed to take forever. Eventually, my name was called and I went to the man at the desk who asked why I could not go to the United States on the visa waiver scheme. I told him I had been to Iran. I had taken my old passport from 1981 with the original visa in (this was before the visa waiver scheme came into place) together with the invitation from the Kessler and other bits and pieces I thought might be helpful. The man said disarmingly, "Ma'am, I just want to speak with you." He was OK and said I would get a ten-year visa and all would be well. I did not have the heart to say I never wanted to go to the States again and was only going because I had already purchased my ticket for New Orleans. After ten days, I had a message to say the visa was ready and I could collect it in Ipswich, which I did. I went to New Orleans but have never been back to the United States since, despite some invitations. Since 1981 I have been to the United States three times a year but have made a vow never to return while Trump is president. I will never forget or forgive the way I was treated. I had better treatment in Iran!

The other thing I should mention is that, as I write this piece today, June 7th 2019, there is something melancholic in the air, disturbing and stressful, as two candidates for the leadership of the Conservative party are vying with each other to see who will be the next Prime Minister who will, in four months' time, be leading us out of the European Union – as they both promise. Mick and I are both strong Remainers and do not look forward to Brexit – which we have fought against for the past three years. To give the reader an idea of how we feel on this issue I am going to quote two letters that Mick has written in the local press. By the end of these the reader will have a pretty good idea how we feel. I should point out that Mick has, for some years now, been conscious of difficulties he faces in debates with others compared with how he could articulate ideas when he was in his seventies. However, he took up writing letters to newspapers, which gave him the chance to debate at leisure and collect his thoughts together selectively rather than muddling in the immediate to and fro of face-to-face arguments.

The first letter

A very old man's thoughts on Brexit

I am shocked when I hear people saying how fed up they are with Brexit negotiations. Their complaints about being bored with arguments, and their expressions of impatience with debate are so stupid, thoughtless and dangerous. If these people were listened to we would simply accept Brexit unhesitatingly on the basis that boredom and fatigue would be alleviated. We would have accepted Brexit simply to make life easier. Plain sailing down to the bottom of the sea!

Arguments for and against Brexit have to be won by painstaking analysis, reasoning, and – most importantly – advice from experts. Where this idea that experts are to be ignored comes from I don't know! Would these same critics be happy with a pilot who has never flown a plane? Would they go to a dentist who has never been trained? Would they be happy with a teacher who has never been educated? Of course not: experts are people who have proven their worth in any particular field or occupation by their intelligence and diligence, by their professionalism and wise practice.

At the time of the original referendum I spent three nights going round estates in Bury St. Edmunds arguing in favour of remaining in Europe. I can tell you that I found this one of the most dispiriting experiences of my life. The reason being that at that time I had no idea what benefits there might be if we remained in Europe. I was entirely ignorant of arguments in support of Remain. My vote in the referendum was ludicrous! The trouble was that this was also true of the Brexiteers who were in a tiny majority, who came to the door and simply shouted "Out" "I want out!" There was no reasoned argument for anybody's vote at the original referendum. That is why it is so important to have another referendum now that we have an enormous supply of reasoned arguments from experts and an abundance of intelligent analysis and discourse that has gone on for two years. We must have another vote, backed this time by informed analysis rather than the superficial prejudices with which we voted last time.

The second letter

I went canvassing at the first referendum for three nights round some of Bury St. Edmunds' biggest estates and at many homes I was told that if we left the European Union we would extend our trade or make new trade with member countries of the Commonwealth that would more than make up for our losses in Europe. Where did this idea come from? It has no basis in truth but many of the electorate used their vote in the belief that it was true! There are countless more lies that were swallowed. But let us stick with this one. Here is a quoted passage from an ex-Australian prime minister reported in some of the national press two weeks ago: "Kevin Rudd said, in answer to the idea that Canada, New Zealand and Australia will be magical alternatives to Britain's current trade with Europe: 'This is the nuttiest of the many nutty arguments that have emerged from the Land of hope and Glory. It's utter bollocks. The combined populations of Australia, Canada and New Zealand of around 65 million does not come within a bull's roar of Britain's adjacent market of 450 million Europeans.'" It's these kind of truths we have come to learn since the first referendum that makes it imperative to have a second referendum. We remainers are not bad losers we want to remain winners economically. Let's get at the truth in a second referendum. Liam Fox has spent two years trying to make deals with other countries outside the European Union. So far, with all the time in the world, he's got nothing significant. In the meantime Europe's agreements with other countries continue to grow, the point being that other countries want a lucrative market consisting of 450 million people and the UK, as part of that Europe, will also grow. It doesn't take a genius to appreciate that the world wants to play with the big boys and girls not the tiny tots! Come on UK, some UK citizens can actually swim to Europe, let's stay with that market.

14 Final thoughts

Life now is pretty good. We talk about Sarah just about every day, we remember her birthday and the two days of her death (the day she died and the day we heard) but we cry much less, we are less dependent on The Compassionate Friends and to use the TCF cliché, "you learn to live with the loss".

Mick and I are both healthy. I still go to the gym several times a week and swim regularly at The Fornham Club. There are people there I see many times. Gillian, a teacher at the school where Rosie and Francesca went, is a good person, whom I talk to frequently; we have the same views on politics. I also like Joan, a swimmer and a keen walker. Beryl and John used to go until they became too unwell. Val is a frequent attender and is usually the first person there in the mornings. There are members of staff who are always ready with a smile including Ollie, Stuart, Ross and Chris. The gym and pool, I feel, keep me sane as well as keeping me fit.

We still travel. I am abroad for work on average once a month and we travel for pleasure four or five times a year. I plan to continue working for at least another three years until our diamond wedding anniversary. I enjoy work and believe that if one stops the rot will set in.

I have tried to make this book an account of both my personal and my professional life. Indeed, the two are intertwined, as I am a spouse, a mother, a bereaved parent, a grandmother, a great grandmother and a clinical neuropsychologist. All contribute to making me the person I am. I believe there are several messages that arise from the writing of this book. First, that one can escape from a disadvantaged childhood. In my case I believe I escaped through education. I went to grammar school and feel this opened doors for me. I do not believe, however, in selecting children at the age of 11 years, even though it worked for me. My own children and both my granddaughters all went to local, non-selective state schools and all did well. This may not be the case, however, in some other countries. My two grandsons in Chile go to a private school as the state schools there are not considered to be good enough. In addition to education I had loving parents even though they often neglected me. I sometimes say I suffered from benign neglect. I was sent to an evacuation home at a very young age without my mother. I was left alone for long periods during the day when I returned to London but neither parent was cruel or emotionally abusive and I always knew they loved me.

The second message is that it is possible to have a family and a successful career. My family is my rock and I love everyone in it but there is no doubt my career has been successful. This would not have been possible without a supportive partner; in my case, Mick, who has always delighted in my accomplishments and done everything possible to back me and ensure my achievements. My personal contributions to success include the facts that I work hard, I am a good time manager, I have never been afraid to fight the system and back what I believe to be right. I am less concerned about furthering my career than I am about wanting the best for survivors of brain injury. At a meeting once on why certain women were successful, we were all asked to give three tips to the young women in the audience. Some of the speakers said things like, "Find a good laboratory to work in" or "Publish in high impact papers." My three tips were: 1. Don't be afraid to challenge things; 2. Do what you feel passionate about; and 3. Make sure you have a supportive partner. I added that we were all working in healthcare because of the patients and not to further our own careers.

The third message is that it is possible to survive the death of a beloved child and to lead a meaningful life even though at the time, one's heart is broken. No parent should outlive their children but, in the end, we have no choice and have to deal with life's blows. Just before writing this chapter (June 2019), I read Nicci Gerrard's book *What Dementia Teaches Us About Love* (Gerrard, 2019). Although writing primarily about dementia, Gerrard has wise words about grief too. For example, she talks about bereavement making time into a torment. Time becomes endless and unendurable. She goes on to say how we, the living, are trapped in bereavement although the dead person is free. She suggests that mourning is a gradual taking of the dead person into oneself. Once exterior the dead person now exists in the minds and memories of those they left behind. The dead person becomes part of us. This is certainly how Mick and I feel about Sarah. Gerrard (who is also the fine novelist Nicci French) goes on to quote Jacques Derrida, who says that surviving is another name for mourning. How true this feels to us. I recommend the Gerrard book to all readers.

These then are my main messages. I hope the book is interesting to read and provides encouragement to those beginning in the field of clinical psychology and neuropsychology.

References

Ashworth, F., Rose, A., & Wilson, B.A. (2018) TD: The case of Diogenes Syndrome – deficit or denial. *Neuropsychological Rehabilitation*, 28, 244–258.

Clark, A.N., Mankikar, G.D., & Gray I. (1975) Diogenes syndrome: A clinical study of gross neglect in old age. *Lancet*, 1, 7903, 366–368.

Easton, A. (2016) *Life After Encephalitis: A Narrative Approach*. Abingdon and New York: Routledge.

Gerrard, N. (2019) *What Dementia Teaches Us About Love* London: Allen Lane.

Gregory, R.L. (2001) Oliver Louis Zangwill. *Biographical Memoirs of Fellows of the Royal Society*, 47, 515–524.

Jelly, A., Helmy, A., & Wilson, B.A. (2019) *Life after a Rare Brain Tumour and Supplementary Motor Area Syndrome: Awake Behind Closed Eyes*. London and New York: Routledge.

Kapur, N., Hutchinson, P., Berry, E., Hawkins, K., Llewellyn, D., & Wilson, B. A. (2009) Executive dysfunction in a case of transoral-frontal self-inflicted gunshot injury. *Brain Injury*, 23, 985–989.

Kime, S.K., Lamb, D.G., & Wilson, B.A. (1996) Use of a comprehensive program of external cuing to enhance procedural memory in a patient with dense amnesia. *Brain Injury*, 10, 17–25.

Laureys, S., Celesia, G.G., Cohadon, F., Lavrijsen, J., Leon-Carrion, J., Sannita, W., Sazbon, L., Schmutzhard, E., Von Wild, K., Zeman, A., & Dolce, G. (2010) European Task Force on disorders of consciousness, unresponsive wakefulness syndrome: A new name for the vegetative state or apallic syndrome. *BMC Med*, 8. doi: doi:10.1186/1741-7015-8-68

Max, D.T. (2008) *The Family that Couldn't Sleep: Unravelling a Venetian Medical Mystery*. London: Portobello Books.

Peters, J.P., Welt, L.G., Sims, E.A., Orloff, J., & Needham, J. (1950) A salt-wasting syndrome associated with cerebral disease. *Trans. Assoc. Am. Physicians*, 63: 57–64.

Pratt, J.L. (2015) *A Notable Woman: The Romantic Journals of Jean Lucey Pratt*. Edited by S. Garfield. Edinburgh: Canongate.

Prigatano, G. & Pliskin, N.H. (Eds.) (2002) *Clinical Neuropsychology and Cost-Outcome Research: An Introduction* (pp. 329–349). Hove: Psychology Press.

Royal College of Physicians (2013) *Prolonged Disorders of Consciousness: National Clinical Guidelines.* London: RCP.

Teasdale, G. & Jennett, B. (1974) Assessment of coma and impaired consciousness: A practical scale. *Lancet*, 304, 81–84.

Tunnard C. & Wilson, B.A. (2014) Comparison of neuropsychological rehabilitation techniques for unilateral neglect. An ABACADAEAF single-case experimental design. *Neuropsychological Rehabilitation*, 24 (3/4), 382–399.

Wikipedia (2019) https://en.wikipedia.org/wiki/Cerebral_salt-wasting_syndrome#cite_note-2 (accessed 16 April 2019).

Wilson, B.A. (1981) Teaching a man to remember names after removal of a left temporal lobe tumour. *Behavioural Psychotherapy*, 9, 338–344.

Wilson, B.A. (1987) *Rehabilitation of Memory.* New York: Guilford Press.

Wilson, B.A. (1989) Improving recall of health service information. *Clinical Rehabilitation*, 3(4), 275–279.

Wilson, B.A. (1999)*Case Studies in Neuropsychological Rehabilitation.* New York: Oxford University Press.

Wilson, B.A. (2009) *Memory Rehabilitation: Integrating Theory and Practice.* New York: Guilford Press.

Wilson B.A. & Betteridge, S. (2019) *Essentials of Neuropsychological Rehabilitation.* New York: Guilford Press.

Wilson, B.A. &Moffat, N. (Eds.) (1984) *Clinical Management of Memory Problems.* London: Croom Helm.

Wilson, B.A. & Wilson M. (2004) *First Year, Worst Year: Coping with the Unexpected Death of our Grown-up Daughter.* Chichester:Wiley.

Wilson, B.A., Dhamapurkar, S.K., & Rose, A. (2016) *Surviving Brain Damage after Assault: From Vegetative State to Meaningful Life.* Abingdon and New York: Routledge.

Wilson, B.A., Robertson, C., & Mole, J. (2015) *Identity Unknown: How Acute Brain Disease Can Affect Knowledge of Oneself and Others.* Hove: Psychology Press.

Wilson, B.A., Rose, A., & Florschutz, G. (2018) Sheehan's Syndrome following Sickle Cell Disease and the story of Natasha. *Neuropsychological Rehabilitation*, 28, 268–276.

Wilson, B.A., Vargha-Khadem, F., & Florschutz, G. (2018) Alexander's disease and the story of Louise. *Neuropsychological Rehabilitation*, 28, 199–207.

Wilson, B.A., Winegardner, J., & Ashworth, F. (2014) *Life after Brain Injury: Survivors' Stories.* London and New York: Psychology Press.

Wilson, B.A., Allen, P., Rose, A., & Kubikova, V. (2018) *Locked-In Syndrome after Brain Damage: Living Within My Head.* Abingdon and New York: Routledge.

Wilson, B.A., Winegardner, J., van Heugten, C., & Ownsworth, T. (Eds) (2017) *Neuropsychological Rehabilitation: The International Handbook.* Abingdon and New York: Routledge.

Winson, R., Wilson, B.A., & Bateman, A. (Eds) (2017) *The Brain Injury Rehabilitation Workbook*. New York: Guilford.

Worthington, A., da Silva Ramos, S., & Oddy, M. (2017) The cost-effectiveness of neuropsychological rehabilitation, in Wilson, B.A., Winegardner, J., van Heugten, C. & Ownsworth, T. (Eds), *Neuropsychological Rehabilitation: The International Handbook*. Abingdon: Routledge (pp. 469–479).

Yee, A.H., Burns, J.D., Wijdicks, E.F. (2010) Cerebral salt wasting: Pathophysiology, diagnosis, and treatment. *Neurosurg Clin N Am.*, 21(2), 339–352. doi:10.1016/j.nec.2009.10.011. PMID 20380974